Recovering Ancient Methods of Bible Study

Anne Kimball Davis

This edition © 2014 by Anne Davis.
All rights reserved. No part of this publication may be reproduced or transmitted in any form or by any means without permission of the publisher.

All Scripture quotations, unless otherwise noted, are taken from the *New American Standard Bible*®, Copyright © 1960, 1962, 1963, 1968, 1971, 1972, 1973, 1975, 1977, 1995 by The Lockman Foundation. Used by permission. (www.Lockman.org)

The *NASB* uses italics to indicate words that have been added for clarification. Citations are shown with small capital letters.

Published by BibleInteract
ISBN-13: 978-1499203318
ISBN-10: 1499203314

BibleInteract
865 Los Pueblos Street
Los Alamos, NM 87544

http://bibleinteract.com

Table of Contents

Introduction 1
Comparing Greek and Hebrew Thought.. 5
Importance of History, Geography and Culture............................... 23
Mysterious Artistry of Biblical Poetry 35
Context and Key Words... 53
Imagery, Symbolism and Metaphor... 65
Symbolism of Names and Numbers... 75
Echoes and Commentary 89
Word Study, Patterns, and Sharing Discoveries............................. 107
Unraveling a Chiastic Construction 119
What to do with a Citation.. 133
Connecting the Two Testaments 147
Stewards of the Mysteries of God... 161
Further Study... 177

Acknowledgements

I want to thank those who contributed considerable time to help me publish this book. Elizabeth Smith reviewed the manuscript and made significant editing suggestions. Faith Benson created the cover and assisted with the editing.

Introduction

You are probably familiar with Christian Bible study, which traditionally appropriates a Greek worldview. This Greek approach recognizes the ability of mankind to perceive universal truths and concepts. In science, for example, these concepts are viewed as mathematical laws. In the spiritual realm of religion, and specifically in the study of the Bible, these truths are interpretative conclusions that declare the meaning of the text. Thus, theology tends to promote interpretations as truth, which leads to doctrinal positions and promotes thousands of Christian denominations, each claiming to know the truth.

This study will take you to an ancient Hebraic approach of searching the Scriptures that uncovers a depth of meaning. This approach understands that the Bible is distinctly different from western literature in two ways. First, it is an ancient text composed in the oriental world. Thus, its worldview is eastern and Hebraic, not Greek and western. Second, its message is spiritual rather than factual, logical and scientific. The biblical message is delivered in an artistic manner that stimulates curiosity, provokes questions, and invites penetration of a deeper understanding that resides behind the plain and simple words.

I was trained in the New Testament with traditional, Greek-oriented methods of Bible study called hermeneutics and exegesis. Hermeneutics is a method of interpreting the Bible that employs established rules and principles. It is generally conducted using English translations. Exegesis is a field of study that critically explains the interpretation, and is traditionally practiced with the original languages. However, in my experience, these approaches to Bible study seem to reinforce pre-existing theological positions, so I found myself feeling unsatisfied and troubled.

Furthermore, I am naturally curious, often resisting a simple answer that merely provokes questions and demands explanation. Perhaps I have never outgrown my childhood curiosity and excitement of discovery. So, I have been drawn repeatedly to troubling passages in the New Testament that have stimulated different possible interpretations, often representing two polar and conflicting positions. I wanted to uncover answers to my own satisfaction. Yet, when I tried to make sense of these different theological perspectives, I was unconvinced and found the methods of hermeneutics and exegesis inadequate and unsatisfying.

My questions began to grow.

- Who will be saved?
- How and when will God's children be saved?
- What is God's purpose and plan for Israel?
- Who will be in the remnant, and what is the role of the remnant?
- Why does the God of the Old Testament seem so different from the God of the New Testament?
- What does the Bible say about suicide…and divorce…and the role of women?

God has used my curiosity to lead me on a merry adventure that is steadily increasing my understanding of God and what He is doing in this world. It all began when I was working on Paul's allegory of Hagar and Sarah in Galatians 4:21-5:1. I was troubled by the numerous interpretations about God's apparent dismissal of Israel, or perhaps of those Jews who did not believe in Jesus the Messiah. I was also startled to discover that Paul was using five metaphors with no clear meaning and also what seemed to be four outright contradictions of the Old Testament. After much thought, and reading everything the academic community had to offer, I finally concluded that Paul was intentionally teasing his audience. These strange and puzzling metaphors and contradictions offer clues to uncover hidden meaning in the Hebrew Scriptures.[1]

My curiosity also led me to ponder the prevalence of citations in the New Testament. There are, in fact, over 300 citations of the Old Testament in the New. With my growing Hebraic perspective, and a love of the cultural and historical background of the biblical narrative, I began to suspect that these

---

[1] I explain Paul's use of these markers in Anne Kimball Davis, *The Law is not a Curse: Paul's Midrash in Galatians* (BibleInteract, 2012), 178-94.

brief citations provoked a larger memorized block. After all, the original recipients of the New Testament epistles were largely Jewish believers in Yeshua (his Hebrew name which I have chosen to use in this study on Hebraic methods). For Jews at that time, the Holy Writings were hand-copied on vellum scrolls, so they were too precious to be owned by individual families. Thus, Scripture was internalized by memorization. This prevalence of Old Testament citations then led me to a logical conclusion that the New Testament was a form of commentary on the Old, and this stimulated my desire to reconstruct likely first century methods of searching the Scriptures.

I am sometimes asked why I selected the period of the first century instead of reconstructing methods of searching the Scriptures from an earlier period of Israel's history. There are two reasons. First, we have a substantial body of literature that dates from about 200 years before Christ to about 200 years after Christ. I was able to use this literature to consider an ancient approach to understanding the Holy Writings. Second, the first century is the time of Yeshua and the composition of the New Testament text.

The purpose of this book is to explain and demonstrate these first century methods of Bible study. A workbook is also available from BibleInteract, which can be helpful in a small group discussion setting. The workbook comes with twelve DVD lectures on four discs, and offers ample opportunity to practice these methods until they become second nature.

You will find that this book (as well as the workbook and DVD lectures) has four primary goals.

- When reading and studying the biblical text, replace a Greek (western) worldview with a Hebraic (eastern) perspective.
- Learn to listen for pneumonic devices, which may be markers that lead to a depth of meaning.
- Appreciate the Hebraic nature of the New Testament and its intimate relationship to the Old Testament (hereafter Hebrew Scriptures).
- Use an online concordance to study original Hebrew and Greek words.

Before You Begin

To fully appreciate this program, which promotes first century methods of Bible study, you should memorize the Hebrew and Greek alphabets. You will find video instruction to aid you in this effort on the BibleInteract website http://bibleinteract.com. You will be learning to acquire a sense of meaning from the original words rather than depending on English translations. After all, a translation is an interpretation.

We also recommend that you read a good book on the customs and manners of the ancient Israelites. In our BibleInteract courses, we suggest *Manners and Customs in the Bible: An Illustrated Guide to Daily Life in Bible Times* by Victor H. Matthews (Hendrikson Publishers).

Another necessary resource is a good Bible atlas, which will offer a sense of geography as well as giving an historical overview of ancient Israel. Here are two suggestions.

> Thomas V. Brisco, *Holman Bible Atlas* (Nashville: Broadman and Holman Publishing, 1999)

> Adrian Curtis, *Oxford Bible Atlas* (Oxford: Oxford University, 2009)

Let me offer one last word of advice. Although I try to explain things clearly, learning how to use these ancient methods to uncover depth of meaning requires a very different way of thinking, and this makes it difficult. So, take plenty of time to ponder and answer the numerous questions when they appear. That is, do not merely rely on my thoughts and interpretations. The purpose of the book is for you to learn the same skills that I am demonstrating. Finally, don't forget that head knowledge must be followed by practice and application or your knowledge will only glorify yourself, not God. Practice makes perfect, and sharing what you have discovered reveals God to others.

Chapter One
Comparing Greek and Hebrew Thought

Your ability to perceive the biblical text from a Hebraic perspective, both in the Hebrew Scriptures and the New Testament, will grow as you persist in your study of the Bible. This chapter will introduce you to four Hebraic ways of perceiving the Scriptures by comparing the Greek and Hebraic viewpoints. We will spend more time with the Hebraic approach, and will consider examples from Scripture.

1. Stretch for the Truth

You have seen that the Christian approach employs a Greek worldview that elevates the ability of mankind to perceive universal truths and concepts. I sometimes explain euphemistically that "Mr. Green claims to know the correct meaning of Scripture and so creates the Green denomination, whereas Mr. Purple holds to a different creed and promotes the Purple denomination." This simplistic example helps clarify why there are approximately 33,000 different Christian denominations.[2] By contrast, there are only three main branches of Judaism – Orthodox, Conservative and Reformed.

There is an explanation for this large number of Christian denominations. Although both Christianity and Judaism agree that Scripture contains spiritual truths, they promote two different ideas about how to arrive at these truths. Whereas Christianity believes it can interpret correctly, the Hebraic perspective sees these truths residing in God, who is the author of the Holy Writings. "Who is man," they ask, "to think he is equal to God?" Instead of reaching a definitive meaning of a biblical word or passage, the Hebraic approach promotes stretching for the truth. The closer one gets, the more intimate becomes his or her relationship with God where

---

[2] *World Christian Encyclopedia*, eds. Barrett, Kurian, Johnson (Oxford University, 2nd edition, 2009). The Center for the Study of Global Christianity at Gordon-Conwell Theological Seminary estimated 34,000 denominations in 2000, rising to an estimated 43,000 in 2012.

truth resides. Thus, the Hebraic approach works to draw increasingly closer to God and to the meaning of what He has conveyed in His Word.

There is a popular joke in Judaism that captures this Hebraic thinking of drawing closer and closer to God without ever arriving at the infinite depth and wisdom of any one passage or even one word. "Wherever there are two Jews, there will be three opinions." This humorous anecdote captures an earnest desire to search for an increasing depth of meaning because Scripture is perceived to be as infinite as God. Such an approach can lead to heated dialogue and debate, sometimes with the intent of challenging a comfortable tradition in order to uncover an even greater depth of meaning.

The New Testament parables contain several accounts of Yeshua in heated debate with the Pharisees and Sadducees. Without understanding the Hebraic approach of searching the Scriptures, I often find Christians concluding that Yeshua was condemning the Pharisees for their "wrong interpretation" and that Yeshua, on the other hand, had the "right interpretation." This thinking leads to the conclusion that, because they did not believe in God's son, the Pharisees no longer belonged to God with the promise of eternal life. I suggest this understanding is both wrong and harmful. The resulting split between Christianity, with its faith in the Messiah, and Judaism, which supposedly fails to believe, has caused untold tragedies over the last two millennia.

Instead, Yeshua was debating with those who had been educated in scribal schools, or who had been trained by recognized masters. These Pharisees and Sadducees were apparently elevated in their own eyes by their traditional interpretive knowledge. In my own study, I have concluded that Yeshua was not abolishing or condemning their understanding but was elevating their traditional and rigid positions to a higher and deeper level of meaning, which he accomplished through heated dialogue and debate.

Let us look now at a specific debate between Yeshua and the Pharisees in Matthew 19:3-11. We read, "*Some* Pharisees came to Jesus, testing Him and asking, 'Is it lawful *for a man* to divorce his wife for any reason at all?'" (Mat 19:3). Note the italics of *some* and *a man*. I am using the New American Standard Version of the Bible (NASB) whose goal is to adhere as closely as possible to a literal translation of the original text. Occasionally the editors will add a word to help clarify the meaning. When they do, they put the added words in italics. Try reading this verse again without the italicized words to sense what the original listeners would have heard.

Before we turn to Yeshua's response, which will lead us to a deeper meaning, we must stop to understand just who the Pharisees and Sadducees actually were. The Sadducees were a Jewish sect whose members typically came from the upper classes. They were educated in scribal schools, and filled many of the prestigious political and religious offices. The Pharisees were another Jewish sect whose members were more aligned with the common people. They welcomed new members from the lower classes, and tended to offer instruction from itinerant masters rather than from scribal schools. Another significant difference between these two sects was their approach to interpreting the Holy Writings. The Sadducees held to a literal interpretation of the Written Law whereas the Pharisees practiced methods of midrash to draw out previously hidden meaning. The Pharisees were largely responsible for the Oral Law that recorded their midrashic interpretations that were passed on orally from master to disciple.

Now let us return to Yeshua's debate on divorce. We read that some Pharisees "came to Jesus, testing Him and asking, 'Is it lawful *for a man* to divorce his wife for any reason at all?'" (Mat 19:3). How, then, were the Pharisees "testing" Yeshua? The Pharisees were demanding to know Yeshua's position on divorce. In essence, they were asking, "Are you one of us, or are you aligned with the Sadducees"?

The following debate gives us Yeshua's answer. We hear three citations from the Hebrew Scriptures and a fourth implied citation. Capital letters in the NASB identify the citations.

> 1. *Yeshua:* He who created *them* from the beginning MADE THEM MALE AND FEMALE. Mat 19:4 citing Gen 1:27.

> 2. *Yeshua:* FOR THIS REASON A MAN SHALL LEAVE HIS FATHER AND MOTHER AND BE JOINED TO HIS WIFE, AND THE TWO SHALL BECOME ONE FLESH. Mat 19:5 citing Gen 2:24.

3. *The Pharisees then asked:* Why then did Moses command to GIVE HER A CERTIFICATE OF DIVORCE AND SEND *her* AWAY? Mat 19:7 citing Dt 24:1-4.

4. *Yeshua:* Because of your hardness of heart Moses permitted you to divorce your wives. Mat 19:8 alluding to Jer 3:1, 13-14.

This is no mere polite discussion. The Pharisees were demanding to know Yeshua's position on divorce. Yeshua responded to the Pharisees' testing challenge with a sarcastic comment that ridiculed his opponents, who perceived themselves as experts in knowledge of the Law. "Do you not know the law?" Yeshua demanded.

The debate was about God's commandment concerning divorce. The Sadducees took a strict, conservative position based on Genesis 2:24. "A man shall leave his father and mother, and shall cleave to his wife; and the two shall become one flesh." The Pharisees took a more liberal stand based on Deuteronomy 24:1.

> When a man takes a wife and marries her, and it happens that she finds no favor in his eyes because he has found some indecency in her, and he writes her a certificate of divorce and puts *it* in her hand and sends her out from his house…. Dt 24:1

People in Israel at that time would likely have been drawn to the more permissive position of the Pharisees. Those who were listening to this debate would have been wondering, "Which position would Yeshua support?"

Yeshua began with sarcastic irony directed toward the Pharisees who considered themselves experts in the Law. "Do you not know the law?" he demanded. Then Yeshua proceeded to cite three verses from Scripture followed by an allusion to a fourth verse. He crafted these four verses in an argument that led to a beautiful and powerful conclusion. Without knowing first century methods of searching the Scriptures we have missed it. Let me now explain how these ancient methods apply to this passage.

Because the Pharisees were referring to Deuteronomy 24:1-4 that permitted divorce for ערות דבר (*ervat davar*, translated "some indecency" in the NASB), Yeshua could take another verse that used the same Hebrew verbal root that is translated "naked" in Genesis 2:25. "The man and his wife were both naked, and they felt no shame" (Gen 2:25). This verse follows immediately after what Yeshua cited and would have been part of a memorized passage by the ancient Israelites. "Feeling no shame" occurred before the fall of Adam and Eve, which was before the introduction of sin. Therefore, Yeshua chose two verses about God's creation of mankind that convey a state of perfection. Look again at the first two verses. They are both from the creation account, and in both we see that God created perfection in mankind before the fall.

> 1. *Yeshua:* He who created *them* from the beginning MADE THEM MALE AND FEMALE. Mat 19:4 citing Gen 1:27

> 2. *Yeshua:* FOR THIS REASON A MAN SHALL LEAVE HIS FATHER AND MOTHER AND BE JOINED TO HIS WIFE, AND THE TWO SHALL BECOME ONE FLESH. Mat 19:5 citing Gen 2:24.

The people of ancient Israel would have known the rest of the verse. "God created man in His own image, in the image of God He created him; male and female He created them" (Gen 1:27). Therefore, in the beginning, the relationship of God with mankind, mirrored by the marriage relationship, was in complete harmony. There was no separation. However, when sin appeared, so did divorce. Sin causes separation between God and His people. Divorce is separation between a husband and wife.

Now Yeshua turns to a certificate of divorce, which appears in the Deuteronomy passage that the Pharisees were using as evidence for permitting separation in marriage. Since the debate was about a "certificate of divorce," Yeshua could then refer to the Jeremiah passage where God gave Israel a certificate of divorce for immoral behavior, but then promised to take them back if they repented and returned to Him. I suggest you stop now and read

Jeremiah 3:6-14 before considering the questions below about this Jeremiah passage.

- Who was King Josiah? Over what kingdom did he rule?
- Jeremiah talks about Israel, meaning the ten northern tribes that were taken into captivity by the Assyrians. Why did God allow them to be taken into captivity?
- How does the term "harlotry" convey the ungodly behavior of the two southern tribes of Judah?
- How did God's certificate of divorce represent separation? What had caused this separation?
- God's certificate of divorce was not permanent. What did the children of Israel have to do to end their separation from God?

"Only acknowledge your iniquity, that you have transgressed against the Lord your God," announced God to His people. "Return, O faithless sons," he declared, "and I will bring you to Zion" (Jer 3:13-14). Thus, God's certificate of divorce represents the separation caused by sin, but repenting and returning to God restores the relationship between God and His people.

Now listen to the harsh words that Yeshua directs to the unrepentant and prideful Pharisees. "Because of **your** hardness of heart Moses permitted **you** to divorce **your** wives; but from the beginning it has not been this way" (Mat 19:8). I have added bold for emphasis. I suggest you read this verse and emphasize the words in bold.

Yeshua was taking neither the side of the strict Sadducees (divorce is not legal under any circumstances) nor the position of the Pharisees (divorce is permitted by God for "immoral behavior"). Instead, he is using this debate about divorce to point to a higher principle. God desires a close relationship with His people. A godly marriage witnesses and reflects the relationship that God desires. A marriage filled with strife and bitterness, which ultimately leads to divorce, conveys the way of the world that separates mankind from their God.

I give you this example of a heated debate among Jews in the first century in order to demonstrate the Hebraic approach to stretching for the truth. Yeshua, of course, was a Jew, a master with disciples who studied the Law. The Pharisees were also Jews who were knowledgeable in the Law and its practical application. The debate was about God's instruction on divorce. The Pharisees pointed to Deuteronomy 24:1-4 that permitted divorce for any behavior that was indecent or naked, meaning uncovered in a sinful condition. Yeshua then drew from Scripture to point to a higher principle. "From the beginning it has not been this way." Sin had entered the world with the fall of Adam and Eve. However, God is now leading and encouraging His people to return to the beginning when God was one with mankind (Gen 1:27) and Adam and Eve were one in marriage (Gen 2:24). "Just repent and return to Me," God announces through His prophet Jeremiah. When God's children follow this path of repentance, they can again be one with God.

2. Be like the Master

Since the Christian approach employs a Greek worldview, which elevates the ability of mankind to perceive universal truths, Christianity tends to elevate the teacher… and the preacher… and the charismatic speaker. These Christian leaders often convey their elevated position by standing higher than the audience on a pulpit or a speaker's platform. After all, they are perceived as the educated ones who have a sound knowledge of Scripture. However, what they are likely announcing is not *how* to search the Scriptures, or *how* they arrived at a conclusion, but their interpretation presented as truth. The role of faithful believers in Christ, according to this Greek worldview, is to "believe" what they are hearing. Questioning the leader can lead to disapproval, sometimes accompanied by guilt as a method of persuasion.

When I encourage my students to ask questions about a biblical passage, they sometimes respond with hesitation and nervousness. Having been raised with a Greek worldview I can understand this hesitation, which reflects two factors. First, they have been taught to "believe," not to question. Second, they expect me, as the teacher, to know the correct interpretation, and they are worried they will give "the wrong answer." I explain that curiosity and questioning is the first step to searching the Scriptures in the Hebraic way.

What, then, is my role as the teacher? Let us review what we have just learned. The Hebraic way is to stretch for the truth by being curious and asking questions that will lead to dialogue and debate. This heated conversation can be carried on not only with other students but also with the instructor. The one requirement is to offer supporting evidence from Scripture.

In addition to helping students search for a depth of understanding, there is another role of the teacher that is our second Hebraic way of perceiving the Holy Writings. You will remember that the Greek approach elevates the teacher because of advanced knowledge. However, the Hebraic way encourages the student to be "like" the master. It is not head-knowledge alone that is important but the way that the teacher has appropriated an understanding of God's Word in his or her life. A common euphemism is "walk the talk."

Of course, knowledge of Scripture is relevant. How else can a person grow close to God? But too often a person stops at mere knowledge and does not penetrate and demonstrate an understanding that leads to wisdom.

Listen to Yeshua who explains, "A disciple is not above his teacher, nor a slave above his master. It is enough for the disciple that he become like his teacher, and the slave like his master" (Mat 10:24-25). I used to think this terse instruction was about pride. That is, if a disciple desired to be better than his master, then he was exhibiting the sin of pride. However, as I grew in my understanding of the ancient Hebraic culture, I came to realize that the focus of Yeshua's words, and the goal of a disciple, is to be like his master – think like the master, talk like the master, live like the master. That is why Yeshua's disciples left their homes and families and followed him. They wanted to be with him so they could learn not only from his words but also from his manner of living.

When it comes to penetrating a depth of understanding, I sometimes tell my students that I am not successful unless they exceed my ability to uncover its mysteries. My role is to show them *how* to expose the richness of Scripture. However, a teacher must demonstrate knowledge with actions. Furthermore, a student should select a teacher, not based on head-knowledge, but on the teacher's manner of living. Then the student should strive to become like the teacher.

The Apostle Paul captures this Hebraic goal of walking like the master with his use of the Greek word μιμητής (*mimetes*) from which we derive the English words "mimic" and "imitate." "Be imitators of me," Paul declares, "just as I also am of Christ" (1 Co 11:1). What a powerful statement. First we find a godly teacher to imitate. Then, as we mature and grow in a close relationship with our Lord Yeshua, it is Yeshua whom we mimic. And when we do, we are walking and talking and acting just like our Lord.

You will remember that when the children of Israel heard God speak from the top of Mount Sinai they responded, "All that the Lord has spoken we will do!" (Ex 19:8). It is the "doing" of God's commandments that pleases God. As we grow in our perception of the Hebraic approach to the Holy Writings, we do not elevate the teacher. We elevate God by walking in His ways as the teacher demonstrates. And, by elevating God we are humbled.

Uncover Mysteries

We have now seen two ways of perceiving the Scriptures that are quite different from our modern, Greek methods of Bible study. First, truth does not reside in any person or creed or denomination but in God. Since God is infinite, so His words encompass an infinite depth of meaning. There is not one black-and-white interpretation. We can only stretch to grow closer and closer to the "truth," which resides in God. Second, the requirement of a teacher is not advanced knowledge but a godly walk that the student tries to imitate.

Before turning to the third way of perceiving the Scriptures from a Hebraic perspective, let me first comment on the approach that uses a literal interpretation. I think you will find that Christian Bible study today, especially in the evangelical tradition, tends to promote a literal meaning of the words. "Just read it and you will understand it," is a common teaching. The only exception is the use of figures of speech, which are literary devices that convey a non-literal meaning. These figures of speech can certainly be seen in the biblical text. However, their non-literal meaning is not mysterious, but quite clear to those who know the rules of these figures that have been preserved in ancient Greek literature. Thus, the non-literal figures of speech become clearly perceived just like the literal meaning of the words.

With the rise of trade, which was stimulated by returning crusaders from the Holy Land, cities began to appear, and a middle class began to emerge that had access to learning in new universities. No longer was the skill of reading and writing exclusive to the clergy. With the rise of universities and the development of the mechanical printing press, the Bible became easily available and a growing number of people could read it. This Renaissance of new ideas precipitated the Reformation that challenged religious traditions.

The origin of this literal approach can be traced to this Protestant Reformation, which began in 1517 when Martin Luther posted his 95 theses that questioned many traditional teachings of the universal (catholic) church. Martin Luther made two powerful pronouncements. First was *sola scriptura* – "only the Bible." That is, those who could read no longer had to depend on theological interpretations provided by the church. With Luther's *sola scriptura* I heartily agree.

Luther's second cry was *sola literalis* – "only the literal meaning." That is, the new educated middle class could simply read the Bible and understand its literal meaning. There was no need to follow the allegorical and esoteric interpretations that had become prevalent in church theology. This *sola literalis*, although initiated with good intentions, led to an understanding that *only* the literal meaning was relevant. Any attempt to uncover a depth of meaning was considered a return to improper and undesirable church interpretation. With this approach I heartily *dis*agree.

We turn now to the third Hebraic way of perceiving Scripture that is different from our modern Bible study. The Hebraic approach to Scripture is quite different from an exclusive literal interpretation. The Hebraic perspective perceives the text as artistic in a way that conveys mysterious shadows and allusions and hints and clues. Those with a heart to grow closer to God will search diligently to uncover this depth of meaning. A person does not need advanced degrees or special training that elevates him or her because of advanced knowledge. Instead, God only sees the heart. Therefore, God will make it possible for these dedicated followers of their Lord to penetrate beyond the mysterious veil of Scripture.

A common accusation by those who insist on a literal interpretation is that "Scripture can mean anything you want it to mean." They resist the suggestion that there is more than just one literal meaning.

Let me stop and explain that the Hebraic approach does not deny a literal meaning, and this literal meaning is often called "the plain and simple meaning," There is a Hebrew word for this plain and simple meaning, which is *p'shat*. The verbal root is פשר (*peshar*), which is used repeatedly in the Book of Daniel. For example, Daniel explained what he experienced in a vision. Then he interpreted the meaning of the four beasts that he saw. Here are Daniel's words. "I approached one of those who were standing by and began asking him the exact meaning of all this. So he told me and made known to me the interpretation of these things (Dan 7:16). The interpretation was the *p'shat*.

With the Hebraic approach, the deeper meaning is often referred to as *midrash*. Again, let me stop and explain this Hebrew word because it is used in several different ways. First, it can refer to books of midrash in the Talmud, which are non-legal rabbinic homilies called *haggadic midrash*. Second, the word "midrash" can express legal renderings that solve difficult interpretive questions. Commonly known as *halachic midrash*, many of these legal renderings are found in the Mishnah, which is the earliest composition in the Talmud. Third is the way that I am using the term "midrash." I am referring to ancient "methods" of searching the Scriptures to uncover its depth of meaning. These methods led to the legal renderings that became known as "laws."

Since you are learning to view the Hebrew Scriptures with Hebraic eyes, you might be interested to know that the term "midrash" comes from the verbal root דרש (*darash*) which means to seek or inquire. You may recognize these wonderful words, "Seek the Lord your God, and you will find Him if you search for Him with all your heart and all your soul" (Dt 4:29). "Search" is our word *darash*.

Thus, the Hebraic approach uses methods of midrash to uncover a depth of meaning in Scripture. As I grew in my understanding of these methods of midrash, I realized that they were typically taught in scribal schools. Thus, the common people would not have been familiar with their use. Instead, they would only have known the conclusions that the methods produced. In this study we will not examine these methods of midrash, which I consider an advanced study. Rather, this study is focused on the common people in ancient Israel, who would have been led to a deeper understanding by "hearing" linguistic devices that acted as clues.

As I better understood the Holy Writings, both the Old and New Testaments, I came to realize that common people in Israel were not left without an ability to penetrate a depth of meaning in Scripture. The more I began to "think Hebrew" as I continued to study the biblical languages, the more I realized that biblical Hebrew is filled with linguistic and pneumonic devices that would have startled the ancient listeners. After all, there were no printing presses, and the Holy Writings had to be hand copied. So, people did not have books or Bibles as we do today. Instead, they memorized from the time they were small children. Therefore, they heard these linguistic devices that guided them to deeper understanding. This particular study will deal exclusively with "listening to the text" in order to respond as the people of ancient Israel would have been led to a depth of meaning. We will leave haggadic and halachic midrash for a later study.

Because the people believed that God had placed a depth of meaning in Scripture that could be uncovered by those with a heart to know Him, they often referred to this deeper meaning as "mysteries." For example, we see the concept of mysteries in the letter to the Ephesians. "When you read [this letter] you can understand my insight into the mystery of Christ" (Eph 3:4). That is, Yeshua of Nazareth did not meet the expectations of the people of his time, so the author of Ephesians was searching the Scriptures to uncover its depth of meaning about the crucifixion and resurrection. I suggest we also should know how to penetrate these mysteries. This you will begin to do when you learn to think Hebrew, not Greek, and you "listen" to the text for anything strange or startling that acts as a clue to deeper meaning.

To further convince you that there are mysteries in Scripture, I will take you now to an account recorded in the Gospel of Matthew. Yeshua had just finished talking to a crowd that had come to hear him speak. His disciples then gathered around and asked him to explain the deeper meaning of the parable. As Yeshua began, he pointed to the crowd and said to his disciples:

> To you [disciples] it has been granted to know the mysteries of the kingdom of heaven, but to them [pointing to the crowd] it has not been granted.
> For whoever has, to him *more* shall be given, and he will have an abundance; but whoever does not have, even what he has shall be taken away from him.
> Therefore I speak to them [the crowd] in parables; because [alluding to Is 6:9-10] while seeing they do not see, and while hearing they do not hear, nor do they understand. Mat 13:11-13

I suggest that you stop and read this account in Matthew 13:1-23. What you find will be provocative. What appears to be a simple explanation in verses 18-23 is crafted with mysterious and artistic language. Furthermore, the so-called "explanation" follows a puzzling allusion from Isaiah 6:9-10 that seems to have no meaningful connection to the parable. Therefore, the mystery to which Yeshua is referring will take work to uncover.

Sometimes my students respond with a feeling of inadequacy. "Who are we to think that we can become disciples who can unravel these mysteries?" However, I explain that Yeshua declared to his disciples, "simply follow me." The original Greek word that has been translated "follow" conveys a vivid and meaningful picture. The Greek is ἀκολουθέω (*akoloutheo*), which originates from a word that means a road or way. Thus, Yeshua is saying, in essence, if you desire to walk in the way that I walk, just follow me and you will become my disciple.

This understanding, that God's Word contains mysteries that can be uncovered by those with a heart to know God, is related to the Hebraic understanding of Scripture. Since God is the author, God's Word will be as deep and infinite as God. Thus, God has embedded mysteries in the depth of Scripture that He will cause to be uncovered in His time.

If you have read this far, you are undoubtedly a disciple of your Lord Yeshua. The goal of this book is to explain and demonstrate the way that people at the time of Yeshua penetrated the depth of Scripture and uncovered its mysteries.

4. Listen for Anything Unusual

In Israel at the time of Yeshua, people did not have Bibles like we do today. The Holy Writings were hand-copied on vellum scrolls and stored in the synagogues. They were too costly to be owned by individual families, so Scripture was first internalized at home by memorization. Later the boys would receive instruction in the synagogue where they learned how to read the scrolls, but they already knew much of the Holy Writings before they began this instruction.

Memorization develops listening skills to a very high degree. Our own schools typically do not teach through memorization today. Instead, our educational system is analytical. No wonder our young people sometimes have trouble listening and concentrating for any extended period of time.

Our modern, western culture absorbs information largely with our eyes, whether through books, or television, or the computer. Even when we enjoy TV, we are primarily watching, not listening in depth to what is being spoken. In ancient Israel they learned by listening, so the biblical text is filled with linguistic devices that people would have "heard." Although these devices are pneumonic tools that aid in memorization, they also act as clues to deeper meaning. We remember that the biblical text is artistic in a way that conveys mysterious shadows and allusions and hints and clues. These pneumonic devices are essential to our ability to uncover the mysterious nature of Scripture.

At this point I will list some of these linguistic devices that you must learn to "hear." Do not try to remember them now. Simply read through the list and consider each one. As you proceed through this book, you will be learning about each of these devices. I will periodically interrupt the flow of instruction to pose questions that will help you practice your new skills. Do not omit these questions or pass over them too lightly. Stop and consider your own thoughts before continuing.

As mentioned earlier, a workbook is also available that will allow you to practice your listening skills and your Hebraic response to anything strange or startling. In this way, you will be learning to think with a Hebraic worldview, and you will begin to uncover a depth of meaning from Scripture that is available to all those with a heart to grow closer to God.

Listening to the Text		
Repetition	Context	Symbolism
Something strange or puzzling	How to identify key words	Symbolism of names & numbers
Parallel lines of Hebrew poetry	Look up the meaning of original Greek and Hebrew words	Echoes and allusions to other parts of Scripture
Chiasm	Imagery	Prophetic language
What to do with a citation	Connecting the two testaments	Extreme exaggeration
Use an online concordance for a word study	Metaphor, an extended symbol	Irony that can be sarcasm, ridicule or humor

To whet your appetite, and to give you an introduction to listening to the text, let us stop for a moment and consider the strange and puzzling nature of the text that appears periodically in Scripture, which I have come to conclude will invariably lead to deeper meaning. These provocative passages serve two functions. First, we are startled by anything that does not seem to fit our understanding of God as He has revealed Himself in His Word. When this happens, we must stop and ponder whatever has caught our attention, which we do by asking questions. Second, embedded in the mysterious language will be clues to lead you to some deeper meaning. The clue will typically take the form of a linguistic device such as repetition, contrast, or a play-on-words. Examples of a play-on-words are synonyms, homonyms, or two words sounding the same but having different meanings.

We will practice with a homonym. You undoubtedly know that a synonym is two words with the same or similar meaning. However, you may not be familiar with a homonym, which is one word with two different meanings. The use of homonyms is common in Scripture, and allows a play-on-words that leads to deeper meaning. An example is Pharaoh's dream about cows and Joseph's interpretation. First there were seven sleek and fat cows, and then seven that were ugly and gaunt. Joseph interpreted this as seven prosperous years followed by seven years of famine. However, what is the word-play in the homonyms?

The Hebrew word for cows is פרות (*parot*). The same verbal root for "cows" is also used for the word "fruit" (פרי *p'ri*). The play-on-words uses "cows" to lead us to "fruit." Furthermore, the Hebrew word for "fruit" conveys three symbolic meanings – an abundance at the end of times when God's people will be with Him, an abundance that God bestows on His people in their daily lives when they are walking in righteousness, and the fruit that we bear for God when we are walking in righteousness. The Joseph story encompasses all three of these meanings for "fruit." First, Joseph is a "type" of Christ who points forward prophetically to the coming Messiah and the end of time. Second, Joseph rescues his brothers from death by famine and brings them to the Nile delta where crops grow in abundance. As for bearing fruit, which is the third way that "fruit" is used, God bestows the inheritance of the birthright on Joseph because he is bearing fruit for God (1 Chr 5:1).

Another example of an artistic linguistic device is irony, which says one thing but actually means another. A common expression to describe irony is "tongue in cheek." We know what is meant even though it expresses something quite different.

I sometimes give this example of irony. A family is eating spaghetti for dinner. The younger brother has his face close to the plate, and he is sucking noodles into his mouth with a loud slurping noise. His older sister exclaims, with disgust, "Pigs snuff slops from a pig sty." She is talking about the way pigs eat, but she is really referring to her younger brother.

Irony can take the form of sarcasm, which is somewhat subtle, or ridicule that is more direct. The older sister was ridiculing the younger brother. We have also heard Yeshua using ridicule against the Pharisees in his debate about divorce.

> Have you not read the law....? Mat 19:4
> Because of **your** hardness of heart, Moses permitted **you** to divorce **your** wives; but from the beginning it has not been this way. Mat 19:8

Ironic sarcasm and ridicule are not acceptable in our modern culture, but was commonly employed in the ancient world during heated discussion and debate. Irony is found frequently in Scripture. Because sarcasm and ridicule are not acceptable today, we tend to perceive irony in Scripture as condescending and judgmental instead of instruction, which was its purpose in the ancient world.

Let us look at another example of ironic ridicule in Scripture. Some scribes and Pharisees came to Yeshua and challenged him to perform some dramatic spiritual action. Yeshua responded by insinuating that they were "an evil and adulterous generation."

> Some of the scribes and Pharisees said to Him, "Teacher, we want to see a sign from You."
> But He answered and said to them, "an evil and adulterous generation craves for a sign; and *yet* no sign will be given to it but the sign of Jonah the prophet." Mat 12:38-39

This ridicule is a form of instruction. Yeshua was not condemning the scribes and Pharisees for questioning his authority, but was offering them (and others who were listening) some powerful prophetic words of instruction. Listen to Yeshua's words that follow his startling ridicule. "Just as Jonah was three days and three nights in the belly of the sea monster, so will the Son of Man be three days and three nights in the heart of the earth" (Mat 12:40). Perhaps some who heard Yeshua speak these words later received an extraordinary insight when he was resurrected out from the dead.

As you progress in your ability to search the Scriptures with a Hebraic worldview, you will be encouraged to "think Hebrew, not Greek." You will learn to "listen to the text," and you will find yourself increasingly curious about where these linguistic devices will lead you. You will be uncovering a depth of understanding that will be life-changing.

However, let me offer a word of caution. You must keep in mind the instruction and warnings of Paul and Yeshua. God will be revealing mysteries from the depth of His Word, but you must become stewards of these mysteries and use them wisely.

> *Paul*: Let a man regard us in this manner, as servants of Christ and stewards of the mysteries of God. 1Co 4:1

A steward guards the information and wisdom that the Lord reveals. Furthermore, this depth of understanding is for the benefit of God's people, so the disciple must serve wisely under the authority of the Lord Yeshua.

> *Yeshua*: Whoever has, to him *more* shall be given; and whoever does not have, even what he has shall be taken away from him. Mk 4:25

In the context in which Yeshua delivered these thought-provoking words, he was speaking not to all who came to hear him but to "his followers, along with the twelve" (Mk 4:10). Thus, Yeshua is also directing this advice to you as well. If you are wise in your use of the information you will be uncovering, then the Lord will show you more…and more…and more.

Chapter Two
Importance of History, Geography and Culture

The goal of this book is to immerse you in Israel at the time of Yeshua so you will begin to think about the Scriptures in the same way as the ancient Israelites. To do this you must become fully informed about the geography of the land and the history and culture of the people. Although this is not a course on history, geography or culture, I will take time now to demonstrate from Scripture the importance of this information for your study of the Bible.

In the introduction I recommended that you read a good book on the customs and manners of the ancient Israelites. In our BibleInteract courses, we suggest *Manners and Customs in the Bible: An Illustrated Guide to Daily Life in Bible Times* by Victor H. Matthews. It is also essential that you have a good Bible atlas that will offer not only a sense of geography but also an historical overview of ancient Israel. Here are two suggestions you may wish to consider. *Holman Bible Atlas* by Thomas V. Briscoe and *The Oxford Bible Atlas* by Adrian Curtis.

I will now offer you some examples of the importance of knowing the geography, history and culture of ancient Israel as you learn to uncover mysteries in Scripture.

Who were the Philistines? Importance of Geography

The Philistines were a pagan people who lived on the coastal plain of the land of Canaan just south of what is today Tel Aviv. The biblical narrative portrays their presence during the Period of the Judges, and they became Israel's hostile enemy. To appreciate the accounts of Samson and the Philistines, Saul and the Philistines, and David and the Philistines, you must understand why the Philistines were such troublesome neighbors.

In a Bible atlas you will learn that the Philistines came originally from the islands of the Aegean Sea, which lies between Greece and Turkey. Archaeologists have drawn this conclusion from the similarity of the pottery style and decoration. Because they came from across the sea, the Philistines were known as "the sea people."

Something caused the Philistines to be dislodged from their traditional homeland, but scholars offer different suggestions. In any case, we have found evidence of their landing on the western coast of Turkey, fighting a sea battle with the Egyptians, and finally settling on Israel's coastal plain. In a Bible atlas you will see that the location of the Philistines on the coast of Israel was significant because they had settled along the major trade route between Mesopotamia to the north (the land between the Tigris and Euphrates Rivers which is Iraq today) and Egypt to the south. Their alliance with Egypt, and the wealth they earned from trade, made them a powerful threat to the Israelites who were living in the central hill country.

The Philistines were ruled by five lords, each one controlling a walled city and its surrounding territory. Archaeologists have identified these sites, and have conducted excavations that have significantly increased our knowledge of these sea people. The five Philistine city-states were Ashdod, Ashkelon, Gaza, Ekron and Gath. You may remember that the giant Goliath, who was killed by young David, came from Gath.

In contrast to the powerful walled cities occupied by Philistines, the Israelites lived in small villages that had no protective walls. Farming was an arduous process requiring terraces on the hillsides, storing rain water in cisterns, and building an intricate system of irrigation.

I suggest you stop now and use your Bible atlas to identify the following:

- Israel's hill country where the Israelites settled after entering the land of Canaan
- The area occupied by the Philistines
- Mesopotamia (the land between the Tigris and Euphrates Rivers)
- Egypt
- The trade route between Mesopotamia and Egypt that passed through the land of the Philistines
- The five Philistine cities

Samson and the Philistines

When the twelve tribes of Israel settled in the land of Canaan, each tribe was allocated a different portion of land. The tribe of Dan was given the area west of Jerusalem that extended from the central hill country to the coastal plain on the Mediterranean Sea. The Danites were unable to conquer the Philistines, who lived in the coastal plain, so they settled in the land immediately adjacent to their powerful neighbors where the ground begins to rise into the hill country.

Samson came from the tribe of Dan and lived in the small Israelite village of Timnah. The story of Samson represents the conflict between the Philistines and the Israelites, and demonstrates the power of God to overcome the enemy of His people. As a result of Samson's single-handed encounters with the Philistines, this enemy was so weakened that the unification of the twelve tribes could occur under Saul, David and Solomon.

The story of the tribe of Dan is an interesting one. Because they lived so close to the powerful Philistines, they found themselves in a tenuous position that was hard to defend. Sometime after the exploits of Samson, they migrated north and conquered Laish, an outpost of the Phoenician city-state of Sidon, which was too far from Laish to come to their defense as we read in Judges 18.

I suggest you turn now to your Bible atlas and locate Laish, which was conquered by the Danites. Also identify Sidon and the area settled by the Phoenicians. You will see why the tribe of Dan was able to occupy Laish.

Saul and the Philistines

Saul was chosen as the first king of Israel. He and his son, Jonathan, and Jonathan's close friend, David, fought valiant battles against the Philistines.

One of my favorite stories involves the courage of Jonathan, who single-handedly generated such enthusiasm and confidence among Saul and his army that an Israelite victory could be won despite overwhelming odds. The story appears in 1 Samuel 14.

I have visited the site of this battle at Michmash, which is located north of Jerusalem in the Palestinian area, and I could visualize the exploits of Jonathan. There is a narrow valley that runs between two high ridges. The Israelites were on one ridge, and the Philistine army was camped on the other. Scripture describes it as follows. "Between the passes by which Jonathan sought to cross over to the Philistines' garrison, there was a sharp crag on one side, and a sharp crag on the other" (1 Sam 14:4).

Under the cover of darkness, Jonathan and his armor bearer crossed over the valley to the opposite ridge. They found a cleft in the cliff that allowed them to climb to the top of the ridge where the Philistines were camped. Their sudden and unexpected appearance so startled the small number of Philistines on guard, that they were able to kill and rout these soldiers. When Saul and his army saw the valiant fight of Jonathan and his armor-bearer, they joined the fight and defeated the Philistines.

Unfortunately, Saul and Jonathan ultimately met their deaths at the hand of the Philistines on Mount Gilboa, which is situated at the northern edge of the hill country. Although camped in the hills above the Jezreel Valley, this location failed to offer sufficient protection for the army of Israel. The Philistines marched up into the hill country from Beit She'an, the walled city in the Jezreel Valley that they occupied at the time. The Philistines hung the bodies of Saul and Jonathan on the walls of Beit She'an, although brave Israelite soldiers recovered their bodies in the darkness of the night. Proper burial was important to the Israelites.

I suggest you stop now to read about Saul and the Philistines in your Bible atlas. Then locate the following:

- Elah Valley were David fought Goliath
- Michmash where the brave action of Jonathan led the Israelites to a victory over the Philistines
- Mount Gilboa where Saul and his army were ultimately defeated by the Philistines
- Beit She'an, the walled city controlled by the Philistines that was located on the trade route

Historical Background for the Prophet Isaiah

We love the Book of Isaiah. The New Testament cites Isaiah numerous times about God's promise of a Messiah, and we have learned to cherish the words of this Old Testament prophet.

"'Comfort ye, Comfort ye, My people,' saith the Lord" (Is 40:1; KJV). I am citing from the King James Version because that is what I learned as a child, and these words of comfort are still with me today.

However, did you know that the Book of Isaiah covers three different periods of time? To fully appreciate the wonderful messages that Isaiah conveys, we must know the historical background for these three periods. Each one conveys a different message that is related to the events of the time. Therefore, it is important to know the historical background for each section of the Book of Isaiah.

Chapters	History	Message
1-39	Assyrians conquer the ten northern tribes of Israel, but God rescues the two southern tribes of Judah.	Language of God's wrath and judgment. Repent or suffer worldly consequences.
40-55	After 130 years as a vassal state under the Assyrians, the Babylonians conquer the two southern tribes of Judah and take them into captivity in Babylon.	Language of comfort and encouragement. God will send a Messiah, who will defeat the enemy and initiate God's kingdom.
56-66	The Persians conquer the Babylonians and allow the people of Judah to return to Jerusalem. However, only a small remnant decides to return.	Instructions to a remnant that returns to the land. God offers a glimpse of the glorious future to help them stand firm now.

Let us listen to the first message of wrath and judgment as the Assyrians were approaching the northern kingdom of Israel. This message is for the purpose of encouraging repentance, so it is important to understand that God is not the author of pain and suffering. Instead, God allows His people to bear worldly consequences for their ungodly actions. In this way, God's language of wrath and judgment becomes a form of instruction that urges His people to turn to Him. Read this verse aloud, and listen to the poetic rhythm that evokes a strong emotional response.

> Alas, sinful nation,
>> People weighed down with iniquity,
>> Offspring of evildoers,
>> Sons who act corruptly!
> They have abandoned the Lord,
> They have despised the Holy One of Israel,
> They have turned away from Him. Is 1:4

God is encouraging His people to return to Him by confronting them with their ungodly ways. The poetic rhythm is powerful, and the expanding description of their sinful ways digs deeply into a repentant heart. God cries to His "people" and His "offspring" and His "sons." If this is not enough, the repetitive power of "they" then penetrates the depth of one's conscience.

> They have abandoned the Lord,
> They have despised the Holy One of Israel,
> They have turned away from Him.

This message in the first section of Isaiah (chapters 1-39) is calling the people to repent and turn to God. Only then will God be able to deliver them from the fierce and evil Assyrians.

Your historical atlas will tell you what happened, which I suggest you stop and read now. The ten northern tribes of Israel were taken into captivity by the Assyrians and dispersed around the Assyrian Empire. However, God rescued the two southern tribes.

I suggest you also read 2 Kings 18:6-19:7, and then ponder the questions below about God's deliverance of Judah from the Assyrians. You will be practicing the Hebraic approach of digging deeper by asking and answering questions.

- In your Bible atlas, locate Samaria, the capital city of the northern kingdom of Israel.
- Also find the city of Jerusalem, which was the capital of the southern kingdom known as Judah.

Importance of History, Geography and Culture | 29

- According to the biblical account, why did the ten northern tribes fall to the Assyrians?
- Who were the Samaritans?
- How and why did the Samaritans adopt the beliefs and rituals of Judaism?
- Why did the Jews look down on the Samaritans with contempt?
- What do you think are the characteristics of Hezekiah's prayer that led God to hear and respond by delivering the people of Judah?
- How did God deliver the southern kingdom of Judah?

We turn now to the second section of Isaiah, which occupies chapters 40-55, and records a time that occurred about 130 years after the events of first Isaiah. During this interim period the Assyrians were conquered by the Babylonians, who then occupied Mesopotamia and the land around the Tigris and Euphrates Rivers. As the Babylonians were expanding their empire, they had their sights on conquering Egypt, which meant they had to pass through Judah whose capital was Jerusalem. This time Judah was conquered by the Babylonians, and the two southern tribes of Judah and Benjamin were taken into captivity to the city of Babylon.

There is a significant difference between the two captivities. The ten northern tribes of Israel were dispersed by the Assyrians throughout their empire, so the people were unable to stay together as a unified community. They are called the "Ten Lost Tribes." The two southern tribes, on the other hand, were all taken to the city of Babylon where they continued to live as a cohesive people. This second exile is called the "Babylonian Captivity."

Chapters 40-55 of Isaiah were composed at the end of the Babylonian rule in Mesopotamia. The two southern tribes of Judah and Benjamin had been in captivity in Babylon for seventy years, and a new power was rising to the north in what is today Iran. These were the Persians, and they too were expanding their empire. As the Persians approached the city of Babylon, the Jews were experiencing extreme fear and trepidation. The Babylonians had not treated them harshly as conquered slaves, but had allowed them to create lives for themselves in and around Babylon. But now, an enemy was approaching, and in the ancient world this meant rape and slaughter.

At this point in the historical background of second Isaiah, we hear God speak loving words of comfort and encouragement. His people had been in exile in Babylon for seventy years. But now, declared God, the Persians were going to treat them kindly, and would allow them to return to the land of Israel. Listen to the wonderful words of God.

> Get yourself up on a high mountain, O Zion,
> > Bearer of good news;
> Lift up your voice mightily, O Jerusalem,
> > Bearer of good news;
> Lift *it* up, do not fear.
> Say to the cities of Judah, "Here is your God!"
>
> Behold, the Lord God will come with might,
> > With His arm ruling for Him.
> Behold, His reward is with Him
> > And His recompense before Him.
>
> Like a shepherd He will tend His flock,
> > In His arm He will gather the lambs
> > And carry *them* in His bosom;
> He will gently lead the nursing *ewes*. Is 40:9-11

The third section of Isaiah speaks to a remnant that has chosen to return to the land of Israel (chapters 56-55). Most of God's people decided to remain in the city of Babylon under the Persian rule. After all, they had grown accustomed to their lives there, and returning to a land that had been thoroughly destroyed at the time of the Babylonian captivity was a daunting task. Those who chose to return had to leave behind the worldly comforts to which they have grown accustomed in Babylon. They had to face hunger and hardship as they worked to rebuild the devastated city of Jerusalem in the face of a surrounding and threatening enemy. They are called a remnant. And to help them stand firm for God in the face of extreme adversity, God gives them a glimpse of the glorious future.

> Lift up your eyes round about and see;
>> They all gather together,
>> They come to you.
> Your sons will come from afar,
> And your daughters will be carried in the arms.
>
> Then you will see and be radiant,
>> And your heart will thrill and rejoice;
> Because the abundance of the sea will be turned to you,
>> The wealth of the nations will come to you.
>
>> Is 60:4-5

Without an understanding of the historical background of the Book of Isaiah, you will miss much of the incredible depth of the messages that the prophet offers. These messages are as relevant to us today as they were to the people of Israel who faced adversity from the Assyrians and the Babylonians. And then as a remnant they returned to re-claim the land of God.

How did Yeshua Heal? Importance of Knowing the Culture

I have already recommended a good book on the customs and manners of ancient Israel - *Manners and Customs in the Bible: An Illustrated Guide to Daily Life in Bible Times* by Victor H. Matthews. If you already have another good reference book, feel free to use it. But one thing is certain. You must carefully read a good book on the culture of ancient Israel, and keep it close at hand to use as a reference when you recognize in Scripture an account that requires knowledge of the ancient manner of living.

Another option for learning the ancient culture is a self-study program offered by BibleInteract called, "A Window into Bible Times." Dr. Noreen Jacks has recorded eight lectures on DVD, and accompanies these lectures with a thorough and engaging workbook.

I will now offer an example from the New Testament that requires knowledge of the ancient culture to fully appreciate the passage. We read in Mark 5:25-34 about a woman who had been bleeding for twelve years (cf. Mat 9:20-22; Lk 8:43-47). You must identify this malady with the Hebraic tradition that any emission from the body, including blood, was considered unclean. Because one could only come into the presence of God in a clean and holy condition, the nature of this woman's disease was a curse to her and to anyone who came in physical contact with her.

We learn that this woman had "endured much at the hands of many physicians, and had spent all that she had." Thus, we know that she had tried every worldly solution until finally she admitted failure. It was then that she turned to God.

Listen carefully to the narrative. "After hearing about Jesus, she came up in the crowd behind *Him* and touched His cloak." Thus, we see a "crowd" pressing in and around Yeshua. In the culture of that time the disciples would have been closest to their master. Beyond the disciples would have been the men, and on the outside of the crowd would have been where the women were gathered.

The bleeding woman in this story would certainly not have been allowed to push her way through the circle of men. Not only was she a woman, but her uncleanness would contaminate anyone she touched. Such an action could easily have caused her death by stoning. However, her intense desire was to reach this Jesus of Nazareth. Therefore, she crawled on her hands and knees at the feet of the men, who were apparently not aware of her presence, until she was able to touch the hem of his tunic.

Again, looking at the culture of the time, the people believed that those who exhibited the power of God could transfer that power by touching another person. "If I just touch his garments I will get well," the woman believed. However, Yeshua declared a higher principle. As the son of God, he was bringing something new to God's people. Listen to what happened next.

> Immediately Jesus, perceiving in Himself that the power *proceeding* from Him had gone forth, turned around in the crowd and said, "Who touched My garments?"
>
> And His disciples said to Him, "You see the crowd pressing in on You, and You say, 'Who touched Me?'"
>
> And He looked around to see the woman who had done this.

But the woman fearing and trembling, aware of what had happened to her, came and fell down before Him and told Him the whole truth.

And He said to her, "Daughter, your faith has made you well; go in peace and be healed of your affliction." Mark 5:30-34

The higher principle is a powerful lesson. As believers in Christ, we have the power of Christ in us through God's gift of the Holy Spirit (Col 1:27). That gift remains latent until we activate it by our walk of love and faith in Christ (Gal 5:6). Then we learn that not only does our faith make us whole, but we can also heal others as we bring them to the point of faith and believing.

Chapter Three
Mysterious Artistry of Biblical Poetry

I have previously explained that Scripture conveys mysterious shadows and allusions and hints and clues. There is no better way to introduce this artistic nature of the biblical text than through a study of biblical poetry.

Much of the Holy Writings is composed in this literary form. In fact, some suggest that as much as 40 percent of the Hebrew Scriptures is poetic.

Biblical poetry does not rhyme. Instead, it is composed with rhythm that evokes strong emotions. English translations have typically been successful in catching this rhythm. Read the following verses aloud and feel the emotion that the rhythm conveys.

> How blessed is he whose transgression is forgiven,
>> Whose sin is covered!
> How blessed is the man to whom the Lord does not impute iniquity,
>> And in whose spirit there is no deceit!
>> Ps 32:1-2

There is much more to biblical poetry than emotional rhythm. So now it is time to begin listening for the linguistic devices. Did you hear the repetition? "How blessed is he…" "How blessed is the man…" The meaning of the two blessings is similar, but there is a subtle difference between them as I will demonstrate.

Parallel Lines and the Principle of Relationships

In addition to rhythm, the most striking feature of biblical poetry is its parallel lines, which are often created by repetition or similarity. Therefore, two lines are in a parallel construction if there is a clear relationship between them. The relationship can be caused by repetition, but sometimes we hear contrast between the two lines, or a cause and effect relationship.

In Psalm 32:1-2 we heard the repetition of "how blessed." Therefore, we have a parallel construction as follows:

> 1. How blessed is he whose transgression is forgiven, whose sin is covered!
>
> 2. How blessed is the man to whom the Lord does not impute iniquity, and in whose spirit there is no deceit!

The repetition of parallel lines often employs more than repetition. I have underlined the two repetitions below. The first is "how blessed," which is a direct duplication. The second repetition is "transgression" and "iniquity," which are two different Hebrew words with similar meanings. Thus, the concept of sin has been repeated in a more subtle and powerful way by the use of synonyms in this parallel construction.

> <u>How blessed</u> is he whose <u>transgression</u> is forgiven,
> <u>How blessed</u> is the man to whom the Lord does
>   not impute <u>iniquity</u>.

We have now seen that the basic relationship in these parallel lines has been generated by repetition, both direct duplication and the use of synonyms. However, biblical poetry is teeming with all kinds of relationships that weave throughout the underlying parallel constructions. Look again at the beginning of our verse and the visual manner in which I have displayed it.

> How blessed is he whose transgression is forgiven,
>   Whose sin is covered!

There is a dramatic relationship between "whose transgression is forgiven" and "whose sin is covered." "Transgress" is in parallel with "sin," and "forgiven" is in parallel with "covered." That is, God does not forgive our sins by making them go away, but He simply covers them. The sin is still present, but God's grace prevents the sin from causing worldly consequences of pain and suffering.

Now look again at the powerful relationship between the love of God that covers our sins and the joyful cry, "How blessed is he!" When God covers our sin, we are blessed.

Let us turn now to the parallel construction that follows.

> How blessed is the man to whom the Lord does
> not impute iniquity,
> > And in whose spirit there is no deceit!

At first you may not see the relationship, but let your ear listen once more. This time there is a negative statement for emphasis. "How blessed is the man to whom the Lord does NOT impute iniquity." Then, the relationship of what follows is not repetition but an explanation. Our transgressions are forgiven, our sins are covered, and God does not impute iniquity WHEN our spirit (meaning the inner part of us) contains no deceit. Wow! How powerful is that? We began by letting the rhythm evoke emotion, but then we listened for the exquisite artistry of the parallel construction that explains how and when God grants forgiveness.

Now it is your turn to explain in your own words what this parallel relationship conveys.

- How does God grant forgiveness?
- When does God grant forgiveness?
- Why do you think God grants forgiveness?

You must learn how to do what I have just done with the relationships of parallel lines, so let us review the steps of how to work with Hebrew poetry.

- Always start by listening to the rhythm to feel the emotion.
- Then look for the basic relationships that form the parallel lines. A relationship may be formed by such things as repetition, synonyms, contrast, cause and effect, or explanation.
- Practice writing the parallel construction in a way that displays its artistic form.
- Then ponder the beautiful relationships, which will lead to a powerful depth of meaning.

Continuing with Psalm 32

As we continue to work with Psalm 32, I will pose questions for you to consider. At first I will answer the questions after you have had time to work on them yourself. Then I will merely ask the questions and let you practice answering them.

Begin by reading aloud for rhythm and emotion.

> ³When I kept silent *about my sin*, my body wasted away through my groaning all day long.
> ⁴For day and night Your hand was heavy upon me; my vitality was drained away *as* with the fever heat of summer. Selah.

Did certain words tug at your heart? David was "groaning all day." His agony was so great that his body was "wasting away." Did you see that David's crisis was caused by his keeping silent? Are you curious as to how this crisis can be resolved?

> ⁵I acknowledged my sin to You, and my iniquity I did not hide; I said, "I will confess my transgressions to the Lord"; and You forgave the guilt of my sin. Selah. Ps 32:3-5

Now you must listen for words that are connected by the relationship of similarity, which you will hear in verses 3 and 4. You try it first.

Next you must re-write the poetry in its artistic form in order to assist your analysis of the meaning. There is no right or wrong way to do this. I have "heard" cause and effect, so I have displayed the verses in a way that displays this relationship. When David kept silent, he was not repenting of his sin, so the result was his body wasting away. Read the passage again, this time in its artistic form, and reflect on the cause and effect.

> ³When I kept silent *about my sin*,
>   my body wasted away through my groaning all day long.
> ⁴For day and night Your hand was heavy upon me;
>   my vitality was drained away *as* with the fever heat of summer.

The relationship is conveyed by synonyms – "body wasted away" and "vitality was drained away." Therefore, the two lines are parallel because of their synonymous repetition. So, we have an

ABAB construction. Stop now and practice re-writing these lines, but this time label them with the letters A and B.

In the first A line, David is keeping silent all day. The editors have added the implication, *about my sin*, which helps clarify the topic of the passage. David feels the heaviness of his sin, not every once in a while but all day long.

Now we look again at the second A line to discover that "all day" is in a parallel relationship with "day and night." The intensity of David's agony has expanded from "all day" to a continuous torment that does not stop, even for the rest of sleep at night. David may have felt his sin all day, but God's heavy hand was on him both day and night.

Now we can turn to the relationships of these lines. When David keeps silent all day there is a consequence that he must bear. The relationship between the first A and B lines is one of cause and effect. David is bearing physical and emotional consequences for not acknowledging his sin. His body is wasting away, and the heaviness of his sin is causing him to moan and groan.

There are still more relationships of cause and effect. Did you perceive them? Listen again carefully.

> A. When I kept silent *about my sin*
> > B. Your hand was heavy upon me
>
> A. My body wasted away through my groaning all day long.
> > B. My vitality was drained away *as* with the fever heat of summer.

In the first A line, David was not repenting. In the first B line, God responded by placing His heavy hand on David, which represents a form of instruction called "testing." When I sin, I have a mental picture of God removing His "hand of protection," so He is allowing me to bring upon myself the worldly consequences of pain and suffering that my sin has caused. We all sin from time to time, so these are the questions we must face.

- Do we allow ourselves to feel the heavy hand of God that urges us to repent?
- Do we acknowledge our sin and repent?
- Do we understand that "repent" means a desire to change?
- Do we truly desire in our heart to turn to God by turning away from our worldly behavior?

In the next two parallel lines we again see the cause and effect. However, there is a subtle difference that the ancient listener would have heard. In both lines David is experiencing physical consequences, but his groaning all day is causing a fever. He is becoming physically ill.

A. My body wasted away through my groaning all day long.
> B. My vitality was drained away *as* with the fever heat of summer.

Then what follows is a powerful contrast. On one hand we have David who has not repented of his sin and is bearing both physical and emotional consequences. By contrast in what follows, we have repentance and the resulting benefit.

This time you try to uncover the artistic elements, which will lead to a powerful message. Start by reading for rhythm and emotion.

> [5]I acknowledged my sin to You, and my iniquity I did not hide; I said, "I will confess my transgressions to the Lord"; and You forgave the guilt of my sin.

Before you consider my suggestion of the artistic construction of these lines, try to re-write them in your own artistic pattern. I will give you these questions first for you to consider.

- Do you perceive cause and effect?
- Do you see any synonyms? If so, do they create a parallel relationship?
- Do you see two A lines and two B lines?

Use indentations to re-write this passage with four lines that display their artistic form. Label two of the lines A, and the other two B. Try this exercise on your own before considering what I have seen.

Now it is time to examine the relationships between the parallel lines for the deeper meaning that the psalm conveys. You cannot do this until, and unless, you have re-written this passage in its artistic form to show the relationships. I will share with you what I have seen, but remember, you may see the artistic construction differently.

> A. I acknowledged my sin to You,
>   B. and my iniquity I did not hide;
> A. I said, "I will confess my transgressions to the Lord,"
>   B. And You forgave the guilt of my sin.

This time I will not share my own thoughts with you about this ABAB construction, but will simply pose questions for you to consider and answer. In the Hebraic way of learning, it is best to dialogue with a study partner or in a small group discussion. Feel free to add your own questions for discussion.

- In "I acknowledged my sin to You" (A) and "my iniquity I did not hide" (B), what is the relationship between "acknowledge" and "not hide"?
- In "I will confess my transgressions to the Lord" (A), and "You forgave the guilt of my sin" (B), do you hear a repetition? Or is it a relationship of cause and effect? Explain your answer.
- What is the relationship between "acknowledge," "did not hide," and "confess"? Do they mean the same thing, or are there subtle differences? Again, explain.
- What do you think is the full, rich and deeper meaning of verse 6?

> Therefore, let everyone who is godly pray to You in
>   a time when You may be found;
> Surely in a flood of great waters they will not reach
>   him. Ps 32:6

- What do you think is the full, rich and deeper meaning of all three verses, Psalm 32:4-6?

"A Different Way of Thinking"

Did you find the last section on the relationship of parallel lines difficult? Responding to the artistry of Hebrew poetry can certainly be challenging. "It requires a different way of thinking," my students sometimes exclaim. So, before continuing to practice with the provocative nature of Hebrew poetry, let us stop for a moment and ponder how and why approaching Scripture with a first century mind can be so challenging.

Let us start with the culture of the people in ancient Israel at the time of Yeshua. Do you remember? They did not have books, so they memorized the Holy Writings from the time they were little children. And how did they memorize? They memorized by listening and repeating. The people of ancient Israel heard all kinds of nuances in the text. In contrast, we read. We do not listen.

Why do you think that 40% of the Hebrew Scriptures were composed in poetic form? The answer is simple. The rhythm was easy to remember. Furthermore, we know that all of the psalms, which were composed in poetic form, were sung (although the melodies have not come down to us over the centuries). Songs are also easy to remember. These psalms are filled with the strong emotions of joy and tragedy. They express a deep love of God and the intense pain of worldly suffering. How much easier would it have been to internalize the rhythm and the music of a psalm than listening to an exposition of its meaning?

Consider another characteristic of the biblical text that distinguishes it from our modern world. In the ancient world, the Holy Writings were not only God's inspired Word that revealed who He was, but far more important His words were giving instruction as to the way His people should live. The memorized words that had been delivered by God became the center of their lives. When would they plant? Why were the rains late in coming? What were the consequences of disobeying God? How were they to follow some of the obscure commandments? Compare this perspective that made the Holy Writings the center of their lives with our world today. Our thoughts are not continually on God. We tend to pray when we need help. We turn to the Holy Writings during a weekly Bible study session. We worship God once a week in church.

There is one other observation I would like to mention. We have books and study guides, which explain how others have studied the Scriptures to understand what it means. In the ancient world people turned to Scripture as a guide for daily living, and they came to Yeshua to seek answers to practical questions. The answers were seldom direct, but guided them to Scripture where they could uncover an answer.

For example, when Yeshua came to the Jordan River to be baptized, John the Baptist asked, "I have need to be baptized by you, and do you come to me?" In essence, he was asking, "Why are you, the Messiah, in need of baptism?" Stop and consider the depth of this question. The people who had come to be baptized by John would certainly have experienced a multitude of questions in their minds. John the Baptist was offering subtle and incisive instruction about the arrival of the promised Messiah. "Repent, for the kingdom of heaven is at hand" (Mat 3:2).

Let us turn now to the question, "Why is the first century way of approaching Scripture so difficult for many to grasp?" I think the answer can be seen, in part, through the two different ways of perceiving the truths of Scripture. The Greek, modern way is to think there is "one correct answer." When we were working together on Psalm 32, you heard me explain that "I will share with you what I have seen, but you may see the artistic construction differently." This does not mean that we can make Scripture mean anything we want it to mean. When we are listening to the text the way the people of ancient Israel would have heard it, we respond to all kinds of linguistic nuances that stimulate our curiosity and lead us to the depth of Scripture. After all, people of ancient Israel surmised that since God was the author, His Word would be as deep and infinite as He was.

Once, when I was in discussion with some of my students, I asked them what they had perceived in a certain text. One of the students shared a thought that I had never considered before. In fact, the interpretation was quite different from what I had perceived. My intuitive response was an interesting one, and exemplified the depth of meaning in Scripture. "You must have seen something that is related to what is happening in your life right now," I commented. "Would you like to share that with us?" Thus, we do not make Scripture mean whatever we want it to mean. However, God's Word is so rich and deep that it will speak to our hearts when we go to Scripture seeking God and His direction for our lives.

You will now spend more time learning how to penetrate the depth of Scripture by returning to the way people of the first century approached their Holy Writings. We will continue to work with Hebrew poetry because it demonstrates the mysterious and provocative nature of the biblical text.

Artistic Poetry in Isaiah

The books of the prophets are especially rich with poetic passages because the prophets were conveying emotional messages of judgment and hope. We will turn now to a short passage in Isaiah so you can continue to practice listening to the artistry of the biblical language and to uncover deeper meaning from the artistry.

Start by reading for rhythm and emotion. Then compose your own artistic construction in the box below by using indents and letters to convey relationships. Remember, the people of ancient Israel "heard" the Word of God. Furthermore, the oldest written scrolls that have survived to us today have no margins, indents, or verse numbers. So, you will be creating an artistic rendition as an aid to help you perceive the message. We will begin with the first of two verses. Practice writing them in their artistic form.

> [1] A shoot will spring from the stem of Jesse,
>   and a branch from his roots will bear fruit. Is 11:1

- Did you identify the 'stem of Jesse' with the Messiah?
- What was the relationship between "fruit" and "branch"?
- What was the relationship between "spring" and "bear fruit"?
- I saw two lines, and I labeled each with the same letter A. Why do you think I did that? What did you do? Why?

Your artistic structure may be different from mine, and that is perfectly acceptable. However, you must be prepared to explain your composition and, in the Hebraic way, dialogue by proposing your own explanation as well as posing questions for others to consider.

In my artistic composition, I placed this sentence in two lines because I saw a relationship between "A shoot will spring from the stem of Jesse" and "a branch from his roots will bear fruit." At first there seemed to be a similar repetition of "shoot" and "branch." However, on closer inspection the shoot is the early budding of a seed whereas the branch only grows from the mature plant. Thus, we have a relationship of growth from seed to fruit, or youth to maturity.

The same relationship of early growth and maturity continues with "stem" and "roots that are bearing fruit." This led me to stop and give serious thought about Yeshua, because the stem of Jesse refers to the line of David from which the Messiah has come.

- How does the stem of Jesse fit into the theme of growth?
- Isaiah is talking to the people of Israel, not to believers in Christ. What is the message to Israel?
- However, we can take this message to Israel and apply it to our lives today, since believers in Yeshua also belong to God through their faith in His son.
- What do we learn about this process that starts with a seed and ends with bearing fruit? What does the seed represent? How do we bear fruit? Is there significance in the artistic location?
- How does the ministry of Yeshua reflect the planting of a seed that leads to mature fruit? Must we look to the future to answer part of this question? If so, how?

We will turn now to the second part of the passage. Practice again creating your own artistic rendition. Then be prepared to explain what you have done.

> The Spirit of the Lord will rest on Him, the spirit of wisdom and understanding, the spirit of counsel and strength, the spirit of knowledge and the fear of the Lord. Is 11:2

I set apart in the left margin "the Spirit of the Lord will rest on Him" because the rest of the verse is an expansion and explanation of this "Spirit of the Lord." Then I indented as three parallel expressions "the spirit of wisdom and understanding," "the spirit of counsel and strength," and "the spirit of knowledge." I further indented "the fear of the Lord" to set it apart from the five "spirits" for two reasons. First, the expression, "fear of the Lord," is not referring to a "spirit." Second, it appears that "fear of the Lord" is the final culmination and the result of what precedes it.

Did you "hear" the resounding repetition of "spirit"? In the Hebrew Scriptures, the word that has been translated "spirit" can either refer to the Spirit of God, in which case I capitalize it, or to the inner part of a person. When "spirit" refers to our inner part, I do not capitalize it. The spirits of wisdom, understanding, counsel, strength and knowledge certainly come from God, but they are only manifested when they become an inner part of us. But remember, you may have seen it differently, which is perfectly acceptable if you can explain what you have seen and why.

Now we turn to six key words in the expansion of the Spirit of the Lord – wisdom, understanding, counsel, strength, knowledge, and fear of the Lord. Did these words reverberate in your mind when you heard them? You have not yet learned how to identify the original Hebrew words and their meaning, so for now you will only work with the English translation. (However, I hope you are burning with curiosity to learn how to work with the original words, which we will do in the next chapter).

- Start by looking at the parallel relationship of "wisdom" and "understanding" in the first indented line. What is the relationship of wisdom and understanding?
- Now consider the relationship between "counsel" and "strength" in the second line. What is the relationship of "counsel" and "strength"?
- What is the impact of this parallel construction that relates wisdom with understanding and counsel with strength?
- Now look at the relationship *between* the two lines. Do you see the parallel of "wisdom" and "counsel" in lines 1

and 2? What is the cause and effect relationship between "wisdom" and "counsel"?
- Next, turn to the parallel relationship of the words "understanding" and "strength." What is the cause and effect between these two words?
- How have these relationships helped you understand the Spirit of the Lord?

Finally, were you curious as to why I placed "fear of the Lord" alone by itself? I have spent considerable time working to understand "the fear of the Lord," and I believe it is the conclusion to this passage. The fear of the Lord is the final goal and result of living in the Spirit of the Lord. What do you think is the "fear of the Lord"? Explain your answer from Scripture.

Artistic Poetry in Proverbs and Job

There are four books in the Hebrew Scriptures that are composed in poetic form – Psalms, Proverbs, Job (all poetic except for a brief narrative introduction), and the Song of Solomon. Take a few moments to look at these four books in your Bible. Does your translation put them in poetic form? If so, you must remember that this artistic arrangement is the work of editors, so you should feel free to make changes in the artistic arrangement of the verses. After all, the people of ancient Israel "heard" the rhythm, and the repetition, and the contrast, and the subtle differences between the parallel lines. So, there is no right or wrong way to display the artistic arrangement. Simply listen, and compose the structure as you hear it.

I have listed below two poetic passages as the New American Standard Bible (NASB) has translated them. This time I will not share my thoughts, but will only pose questions to stimulate your own curiosity and conclusions.

In the space following each passage, begin by composing your own artistic arrangement, and label each line with a letter to show its relationship to another line or lines. Then ponder the relationships before considering and discussing the questions that follow.

Mysterious Artistry of Biblical Poetry | 49

¹ He who separates himself seeks *his own* desire, He quarrels against all sound wisdom.
² A fool does not delight in understanding, But only in revealing his own mind.
³ When a wicked man comes, contempt also comes, and with dishonor *comes* scorn.
⁴ The words of a man's mouth are deep waters; the fountain of wisdom is a bubbling brook. Pr 18:1-4

- How and why is "separate" a key word in the first line? If you know how to look up the Hebrew word, you can do it now. However, you will be learning how to do this in the next chapter.
- How does verse 1 convey an expansion of "separate"? How would you explain the function of the expansion, and what meaning does the expansion convey?
- Who do you know that fits the description of verse 2? How would you describe this person?
- In verse 3, there is a relationship between two sets of words – wicked/dishonor and contempt/scorn. What is the relationship between the words in each pair, and also between the two pairs.

- Verse 4 is everyone's favorite. In the space below, write your own questions that this passage stimulates. Then consider the answers.

Questions	Answers

Now I suggest that you work on one more passage in Job to continue learning about the artistic nature of Hebrew poetry. Job is talking directly to God after passing through extremely difficult trials and tribulations. First read the passage below for the rhythm that evokes emotion. Then re-write it in its artistic form using indentation and letters.

> [1] Then Job answered the Lord and said,
> [2] I know that You can do all things, and that no purpose of Yours can be thwarted.
> [3] Who is this that hides counsel without knowledge? Therefore I have declared that which I did not understand, Things too wonderful for me, which I did not know.

⁴ Hear, now, and I will speak; I will ask You, and You instruct me.
⁵ I have heard of You by the hearing of the ear; But now my eye sees You;
⁶ Therefore I retract, and I repent in dust and ashes. Job 42:1-6

- What part of the passage is in a narrative form, not poetry?
- What makes it a narrative? What is lacking that would have made it poetic?
- What are the relationships of the poetic lines that you have labeled with the same letters?
- What is the relationship between "asking" God and receiving "instruction"?
- What is the relationship between the Hebraic concepts of "hearing" God's Word and "seeing" God? How is this a requirement for repentance?

I have worked you hard in this chapter, but I believe it is important for you to carefully complete all of the exercises so you can start "thinking Hebrew, not Greek." The biblical text is crafted in such a way that the people of ancient Israel would have heard all of its artistic nuances. They would have been startled and intrigued, which would have stimulated their deeper thoughts and perspectives. We are not an oral society, so we do not automatically react to what we hear. We must stop, and listen, and ponder the deeper meaning.

Chapter Four
Context and Key Words

In the last chapter, I trust your curiosity was activated when I said, "You have not yet learned how to identify original Hebrew words and their meaning." I trust you have memorized the Hebrew alphabet, so you are ready to learn how to look up the Hebrew word and find where it is used in Scripture. That is, you will not be working with an English translation of your word but with the original Hebrew. You can do this simply by knowing the Hebrew alphabet.

After looking up your word in Hebrew, you will then need to read each passage which contains that Hebrew word. At this point you will be reading your Bible in an English translation. However, when you come to your Hebrew word speak it in Hebrew, and always read this word in the context in which it appears in the passage. In this way, you will gain rich nuances of meaning from the original Hebrew word rather than an English translation.

If you have not already learned the Hebrew alphabet, you should stop now and do that before continuing. In this session you will be working with Hebrew words. Starting in session seven you will need to know the Greek alphabet to work with Greek words in the NT. To help you learn these alphabets, you will find training videos on the BibleInteract website: http://bibleinteract.com

Version, Lexicon and Concordance

There are three terms you need to know. First, a version is a particular translation of the Bible. The version I am using is the New American Standard Bible (NASB). I recommend the NASB Reference Bible because notes in the middle margin will direct you to citations and allusions in other parts of the Scriptures.

Second, a lexicon is a dictionary of biblical words. The lexicon typically starts with the translated English word and then gives a definition in English. We will not be using a lexicon.

A concordance lists all the verses where a certain word appears in Scripture. Some concordances start with the translated English word and list the verses where that *English* word appears.

If you already own a concordance, check it carefully. If it is working in English, do not use it.

Whether you already own a concordance or not, I suggest that you become familiar with the online concordance that I recommend to my students, which you will find at http://www.biblehub.com. For the rest of this instructive program I will expect you to use http://www.biblehub.com

I will now walk you through how to use this online concordance.

Step One: Start with a Key Word

You must start with a particular word in a specific verse. Let's say you are reading in Genesis about the fall of mankind. You come to Genesis 3:8 which says, "They [Adam and Eve] heard the sound of the Lord God walking in the garden in the cool of the day, and the man and his wife hid themselves from the presence of the Lord God among the trees of the garden" (Gen 3:8).

Now you are going to have to learn to be curious, and to let your curiosity draw you to key words with questions. For example, consider the following questions.

- Why does the verse specifically say "the cool of the day"?
- Does "cool of the day" identify a certain time during the day? If so, is that important?
- Did something about "cool of the day" cause Adam and Eve to hide themselves?
- What does the Hebrew mean by "cool of the day"?
- The word you are going to look up is "cool."

Let me stop at this point and share with you how I identify a key word. The answer is simple – curiosity and questions. I sometimes compare myself to Curious George, the mischievous monkey of childhood memory. His curiosity may have disrupted the balance of traditional life and customs, but in the end it was always a wonderful learning experience.

I have just given you the most obvious answer to my question, "How do I find a key word." It is curiosity and questions. However, I suggest there is another equally important way to identify key words. If you "believe in your heart that God raised him [His son, Yeshua] from the dead," as Paul tells us in Romans 10:9, then you have the gift of the Holy Spirit in you through your faith in Christ (Col 1:27). The Holy Spirit will guide your curiosity to key words.

Step Two: Interlinear Bible on biblehub.com

Access the internet on your computer and go to http://www.biblehub.com. In the directory near the top of the homepage click on "Interlinear Bible."

Step Three: Using an Interlinear Bible

An interlinear translation displays the original text of a verse on one line and the English translation for each word on another line. In this way you can find the original translated English word, and then you can see the original Greek or Hebrew word for that translation.

However, when you first clicked on "Interlinear" on the Bible Hub homepage, it took you to the interlinear translation of Genesis 1:1 because that is the first verse in the Bible. Our key word is in Genesis 3:8, so type Genesis 3:8 in the bar at the top of the page on your monitor. You can now see a word-for-word translation of Genesis 3:8, which displays an English word below each Hebrew word.

Look for "in the cool of the garden." You will see this is an English translation for two Hebrew words. We want "in the cool."

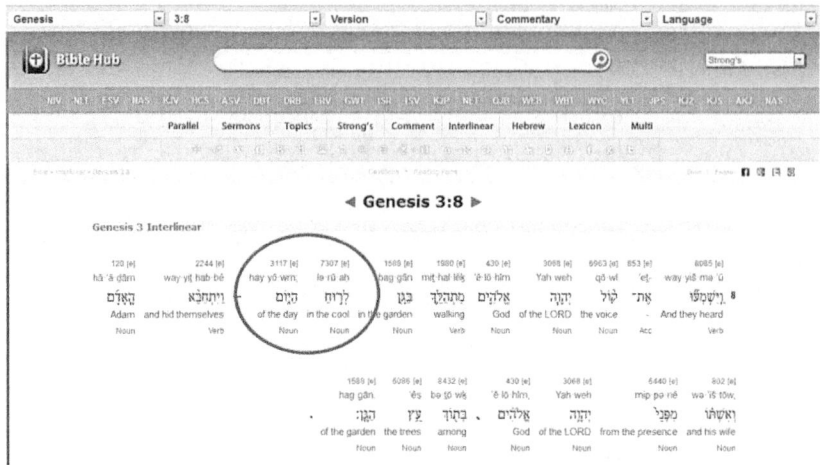

Step Four: Find the Hebrew word

The verse, Genesis 3:8, should now be displayed on your computer monitor. Take some time to carefully examine this interlinear translation of Genesis 3:8.

- Hebrew is read from right to left.
- Now that you know the Hebrew letters and their sounds, try reading this sentence aloud in Hebrew.
- Our curiosity has been drawn to the English word "cool" in "cool of the garden." What is the Hebrew word that has been translated "cool"?

In this interlinear translation of Genesis 3:8, which is a word-for-word translation from Hebrew to English, find your word "cool." You will see that the Hebrew word is רוח (pronounced *ru-ach*). From this point forward, you will be working with the Hebrew word רוח, not the English translation "cool."

Step Five: The Concordance Page

At the very top of your word "cool" (רוח) you will find the number 7307(e), which is the number assigned to this word in Strong's

Concordance of the Bible. Click on this number, which will take you to the concordance page for רוח. You will remember that a concordance lists all the verses where רוח appears in the Hebrew Scriptures. You will see that list on the right side of the page, which is what you will be using to gain a deep and rich understanding of רוח. However, first we will stop to look at another resource on this concordance page.

At the top left of the page you will see that Strong's concordance offers three English translations of רוח - breath, wind and spirit. However, these English definitions of an English word will barely help you understand the depth of meaning of the Hebrew word רוח. Do you really think that English words are going to capture and give you the wonderful, rich essence of the word רוח? And you certainly must be asking, "Why has this Hebrew word been translated into English as 'cool'?"

I often tell my students, "Don't even *look* at Strong's English definition." Why? Because I do not want you working with an English translation. So, what do you do next? You will find the concordance that I want you to be using in a column on the right side of the page. This concordance lists all the verses in which the original Hebrew word רוח appears in Scripture. (Word of advice: you should be speaking רוח aloud, at least in your mind).

Step Six: Using the Concordance

A concordance lists all the verses where רוח appears in the Hebrew Scriptures. That list appears on the right side of the concordance page.

At the top of the concordance column you will see there are 377 occurrences of רוח in the Bible. When there are that many verses, I recommend focusing on the appearances in the Torah. You will also find that the first usage is especially significant. Start with Genesis 1:2, which is the first time that רוח appears in Scripture. Directly below that you will see that the second time רוח is used is in our verse, Genesis 3:8. Remember, you will need to read each of the two verses in their context (surrounding verses) to understand how רוח is used and the meaning that is conveyed.

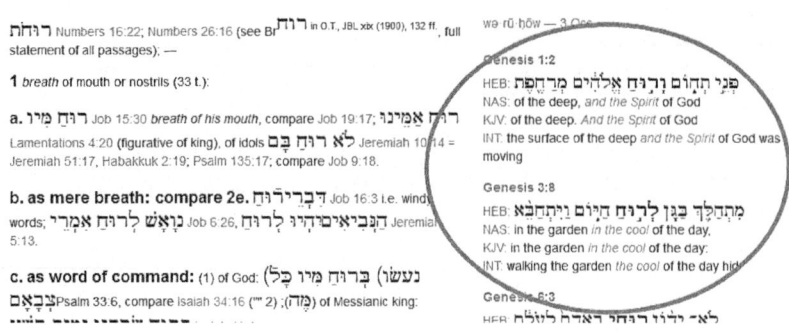

Step Seven: Make a List with Brief Notes

As you read each verse in its context, make a list of these verses. Then write a brief note beside each verse that helps you remember how the word is used in that verse within its context, and the specific meaning that the word conveys.

Since the word רוח appears so many times in Scripture, your list will include only the verses in the Torah. However, as you continue to conduct these word studies, many times your curiosity will lead you to a word that is used less often. When that happens, your list should include all usages of the word. Or perhaps you can scan through the concordance and select the relevant verses that you want to examine.

The purpose of your list is to allow you to review what you have seen so you can uncover some pattern. A pattern is an overall theme. This pattern may emerge as more than one meaning that the word conveys. Or perhaps there is an ascending pattern of the way the word is used from its first appearance in Scripture to its last appearance. Or maybe you will see a contrast between its usage in the first cluster of appearances with the way it is used in the later appearances. These are only examples of patterns. You must learn to review and ponder your list to let a pattern emerge from the details of your notes.

Now it is time for you to practice uncovering a pattern from the word רוח.

- How is רוח used in Genesis 1:2?
- How is רוח used in Genesis 3:8?

- Scroll down in your concordance list to find the next 5 verses where רוח appears. What are these 5 verses?
- Make a list of the first 7 usages of רוח in the Hebrew Scriptures, and write brief notes beside each verse that will help you remember how רוח is used in each verse.
- How and where is רוח used as "breath"?
- How and where is רוח used as "wind"?
- How and where is רוח used for God?
- Now consider how the Spirit of God is like breath or wind?
- What is the pattern or overall theme that you see in these 7 verses?
- You are now ready to return to Genesis 3:8, which is where our curiosity first began. How is רוח used in Genesis 3:8 where it is translated "cool" of the garden?

I trust that this exercise in using a concordance has given you a deeper and richer understanding of רוח than merely the English translation of "cool," or Strong's definition of "wind, breath and spirit."

Before continuing, let us review the steps you have just learned.

1. Let your curiosity lead you to a key word.
2. Use the interlinear Bible in www.biblehub.com.
3. Find the verse in which your key word appears.
4. Click on Strong's number above your word, which will take you to a concordance page.
5. A concordance in the right column will list all the verses in which your word appears.
6. Select what appear to be important verses. Be sure to include the first usage and all appearances in the Torah. Make a list with notes for each verse you have selected.
7. As you review your notes, ask yourself questions that help disclose a pattern (an over-all theme). Finding this pattern will enable you to gain a deeper understanding than the English translation could ever offer.

Key Word in the Cain and Abel Story

You will now have an opportunity to practice what you have studied. We all know the story of Cain and Abel, but now we will work to uncover a new depth of meaning. You are letting your curiosity draw you to key words, and you are using an online concordance to understand the original meaning rather than an English translation.

Before beginning this exercise, stop and carefully read Genesis 4:2-5. Listen to the rhythm and emotion, and stimulate your curiosity by asking questions.

We will now begin with Genesis 4:2.

> Abel was a keeper of flocks,
> but Cain was a tiller of the ground. Gen 4:2

The little word "but" indicates a contrast, which creates a relationship of opposites. If you start listening for "but" whenever you read the Bible, you will find contrast all over Scripture. Typically the contrast is between the way of the world and the way of God, but this verse is mysterious. Why is keeping the flocks a contrast to tilling the ground? To answer this question we must read the verse in its context.

Context simply means the surrounding verses that give one small part of the biblical text a more complete meaning. In this case, the immediate context of Genesis 4:2 is Genesis 4:2-5, which you have already read. So, let us stop now and consider the context of our verse more carefully. Try composing Genesis 4:2-5 in an artistic structure before continuing to read my suggestions.

Context and Key Words | **61**

I trust you read first for rhythm and emotion. Then, did you "hear" any of the following linguistic devices?

- Repetition
- Contrast
- Parallel relationships
- Key words

I will share with you now what I perceived as the artistic structure of these verses. You may have seen something different, and that is perfectly all right. However, be prepared to explain the relationships that you see.

So it came about in the course of time that
   A. Cain brought an offering to the Lord of the fruit of the ground.
      B. Abel, on his part also brought of the firstlings of his flock
         C. and of their fat portions.
   B And the Lord had regard for Abel and for his offering;
   A. But for Cain and for his offering He had no regard. Gen 4:3-5

Now let us practice perceiving the relationship of these parallel lines. In the first A and B lines we have Cain's offering, and we have Abel's offering. The offerings are different; one is fruit of the ground and the other is firstlings of the flock. However, nothing seems to be unusual. Each offering is related to an agricultural task, one of growing food and the other of raising animals. We still don't understand what that contrast is.

The more interesting relationship for me is between the two A lines and the two B lines, which are cause and effect. And, look at the letter C, which sits apart in the middle. The fat portion of a sacrificed animal was the part that was burned as a sweet aroma to God. This is the gift that Abel was giving to God.

Before we turn to identify an important key word, did you hear the repetition? Did you look up the key word that has been translated "regard for"? If so, you have a dramatic visual picture of this unfolding event because the Hebrew word means to look intensely at something.

I will now draw your attention to a key word, which is going to help you perceive the contrast.

- The NASB has used "firstlings" in their translation. What version of the Bible are you using? Is there a different translation of this word in your Bible?
- You might be interested to know that the King James Version (KJV) also translates "firstlings," but the New International Version (NIV) translates "firstborn." Are you curious to know the Hebrew word and what it really means?
- Use your online interlinear Bible at http://www.biblehub.com to find Genesis 4:4. Then identify the Hebrew word for "firstlings."
- Click on Strong's number that will take you to the concordance page. You will see that Strong defines בכרה (*b'chorah*) as "the right of first-born." However, this is an English translation, and all translations are interpretation. So, it is time to use the concordance in the right column of the page.
- How many times does בכרה appear in Scripture?

Now it is time for you to make a list of the 14 verses where בכרה appears in the Hebrew Scriptures. Read each verse in its context, and take brief notes to help you remember how בכרה is used in each verse. Then consider the following questions.

- The Jewish sages believed (and I have come to agree with them) that God marks the first usage as especially important. How is בכרה first used in Scripture?
- Review your notes on all 14 verses of בכרה. How many of the 14 verses refer to a firstborn son who was entitled to the inheritance of the birthright? How many times does בכרה refer to a firstborn animal?
- Since Genesis 4:4 refers to a firstborn animal, carefully re-read the verses where בכרה refers to a firstborn animal.

In the sacrificial system of ancient Israel, animals were given as gifts to God. However, it could not be just any animal. The very best was an unblemished firstborn male. The firstborn son was equally important to the ancient Israelites because this son was groomed to become the next leader of the family, clan or tribe.

You will remember that the tenth plague in Egypt at the time of the Exodus killed all the firstborn Egyptians, both man and animal. Yet, God caused death to pass over Israel whom He declared to be His firstborn son. The unblemished animals the Israelites sacrificed, whose blood they placed on the lintels and door posts of their homes, were accepted by God as a holy sacrifice. As for the Egyptians, the reason the tenth plague so devastated Egypt was because it eliminated all firstborn sons, who were the leaders of their people.

You are now ready to return to the key word בכרה in the Cain and Abel story, which has been translated "firstling" in the NASB. We know that Abel brought "the firstlings of his flock and of their fat portions" (Gen 4:4). That is, Abel gave to God the very best, which was a firstborn animal of his flock. Furthermore, in the sacrificial system of ancient Israel, it was the fat portion of the animal that was burned as sweet incense to God. So, in this wonderful vivid imagery, Abel was offering the best of his flock to God in sacrifice, which would have been the act of a son who was worthy of a leadership role among God's people.

What about Cain? We read that "Cain brought an offering to the Lord of the fruit of the ground." Produce from the field was also given to God as an offering in the sacrificial system. However, can you guess what kind of produce God would have accepted? If you guessed the first fruits of the crop (the equivalent to the first born animals), then you were right. Did Cain bring the first fruits of his produce? That is not what the text tells us, which simply declares that "Cain brought an offering to the Lord." Do you now understand the contrast between Abel, whose offering God accepted, and Cain, whose offering God rejected?

I have just taken you through another exercise of identifying a key word and the use of a concordance to penetrate a deeper meaning. I suggest you develop a habit of daily Bible study where you can use this skill. Select an hour each day that fits what is undoubtedly a busy schedule. Then just start reading anywhere you choose, and let your curiosity draw you to a key word. If you allocate 4-5 days each week to this Bible study, you will have conducted 4-5 of these word studies. You will be surprised at how rapidly your depth of understanding will grow, as well as your comprehension of an expanding number of Hebrew words.

Chapter Five
Imagery, Symbolism and Metaphor

Biblical Hebrew is teeming with language that activates all five senses in a powerful way. The language is terse, using few words, but the imagery is vivid. We can see young David with his curly red hair, arriving from the field where he had been taking care of the sheep. We learn that David was "ruddy with beautiful eyes and a handsome appearance" (1 Sam 16:12). This young boy must have been awed and bewildered as he stood before his father, his seven older brothers, and the judge who spoke for God over all of Israel. We hear Samuel, the judge, bellowing to Jesse, David's father, with his arm outstretched in the direction of young David. "Arise, anoint him!"

Imagery uses vivid and descriptive language to evoke a picture in our minds. Remember, the ancient Israelites "heard" the Holy Writings; they did not read them. So, you too must learn to "listen" to the words that evoke these images.

The Hebrew text is teeming with this powerful imagery. The New Testament Greek text is more cerebral, which is characteristic of the Greek language. However, the authors of the New Testament were, in large part, Jews who knew the Hebrew Scriptures intimately. So, we often find imagery in the New Testament as well. Perhaps the best example of New Testament imagery is in Paul's account of the shipwreck in Acts 27.

Imagery in the Hebrew Scriptures

You will now practice responding to imagery with a poem that is often called the Song of Deborah. It is a "song" because as you read it (or preferably listen to it) you will hear its emotional poetic rhythm. In ancient Israel, these poems were sung, although the tunes have been lost. Stop now and read Judges, chapters 4 and 5.

- Judges chapter 4 is in a narrative literary form. What makes it a narrative?
- Judges chapter 5 is in a poetic literary form. What makes it poetic?

You undoubtedly noticed that the narrative account in chapter 4 is repeated in poetic form in chapter 5. Scholars suggest that the narrative was probably composed during the United Monarchy, which would have followed the Period of the Judges when the event took place. The purpose was to unite the 12 tribes under one king. However, the song in chapter 5 appears to have been composed at a much earlier time during the Period of the Judges, perhaps immediately after the battle when the women would have sung this victory song.

We must stop now to review the geography and the historical background of this story. Use your Bible atlas to answer the following questions.

- The beginning of the Period of the Judges followed what major events in the history of ancient Israel?
- The following tribes play a role in this story – Ephraim, Naphtali and Zebulun. Identify on a map the territory that each of these tribes occupied.
- The enemy in the story is Jabin, the Canaanite king of the powerful walled city of Hazor that was located on the main trade route as it passed through northern Israel on its way to Egypt. Identify on a map both the city of Hazor and the trade route as it passed through Israel.
- How were the tribes of Naphtali and Zebulun affected by the Canaanites in Hazor?
- How and why was the tribe of Ephraim likely isolated from the controlling power of Jabin, the Canaanite king?
- Deborah came from the tribe of Ephraim. How does Judges 4:4 explain that she was speaking the words of God to the people of Israel?
- What does it mean that Deborah was "judging Israel at that time"?
- Deborah, who spoke for God and advised His people, would have been a judge over all of Israel. Review once more where each of the twelve tribes of Israel settled in the Promised Land.
- Deborah called Barak and told him, "Go and march to Mount Tabor, and take with you ten thousand men from

Imagery, Symbolism and Metaphor | 67

the sons of Naphtali and from the sons of Zebulun" (Jdg 4:6). Identify on a map Mount Tabor.
- How did the location of Mount Tabor make it impossible for the Israelite soldiers to run away from the enemy?
- Deborah tells Barak, "I will draw out to you Sisera, the commander of Jabin's army, with his chariots and his many *troops* to the river Kishon, and I will give him into your hand." (Jdg 4:7). The Kishon River was the site. Find the location of the Kishon River.

Now you must stop again, this time to consider the ancient culture of Israel as it applies to this story. You will find your answers to the following questions in the narrative account in Judges chapter 4.

- We learn that the leader of the Canaanite army was Sisera, which is not a Canaanite name, so apparently he was a mercenary soldier. What is the contrast and symbolism of the men of Israel who were fighting under the leadership of their God (through the words He spoke to Deborah), and their opponent who was a mercenary soldier? Based on this imagery, what was going to be the outcome of the battle?
- The Canaanite army had iron chariots, which means they also had iron weapons. How would they have fought the battle?
- The Israelites were on foot with weapons that were not made of iron. How would they have fought the battle?

The Israelites won a miraculous battle against the Canaanite forces from Hazor because God caused the River Kishon to fill with water from a cloudburst in the hill country of Ephraim. The iron chariots became stuck in the muddy bottom of the Kishon River, and the inferior weapons of the Israelites could then be used to overcome the enemy.

Sisera, the mercenary leader of the Canaanite army, fled on foot and came to the tent of Jael.

- What is the symbolic meaning of Sisera fleeing on foot?
- Why is Jael, not Deborah, the heroine of the story?

Jael was a Bedouin whose people lived in tents and migrated from one location to another. The women were responsible for pitching and dismantling the tents of these nomadic people.

Jael was apparently alone when Sisera arrived. She invited him in to her side of the tent (reserved only for women), offered him a drink that would have made him drowsy, and when he was asleep she killed him with a tent peg.

Now we will leave the narrative in chapter 4, and will turn to the song of the women in chapter 5. Listen to the rhythm of the poem, and let the imagery come alive in your imagination.

> She reached out her hand for the tent peg,
> And her right hand for the workmen's hammer.

Read it once more, and get a picture in your mind of Jael who was holding the tools of the women, a tent peg and a hammer for pitching the tent of her nomadic people. She silently took the tent peg, placed it directly above the head of Sisera while he was sleeping, and with the hammer in her other hand she drove the tent peg with one powerful stroke into his head.

> She struck Sisera,
>   she smashed his head;
>   she shattered and pierced his temple.

Now comes the most vivid imagery of all.

> Between her feet he bowed, he fell, he lay;
> Between her feet he bowed, he fell;

> Where he bowed, there he fell dead. Jdg 5:26-2

Between her feet is sexual imagery. Sisera considers himself a powerful warrior whose self-image would have extended to the domination of women. But rather than raping Jael, Jael rapes Sisera. "Between her feet he bowed, he fell." The last line stands alone for emphasis. "Where he bowed" should still be read in poetic rhythm, but "there he fell dead" should emphasize each word as with the stroke of the hammer in Jael's hand.

Symbolism

Imagery and symbolism are two different figures of speech. However, they are often used together, so you need to distinguish between the two. An image is a picture in your mind. A symbol uses a material object to represent an abstract idea.

We have just experienced the powerful and vivid imagery of Jael who killed Sisera with a tent peg and a hammer. These implements were tools used by the women to pitch the Bedouin tents, but they became weapons of war in the hands of Jael. The tent peg and the hammer symbolize the determination and courage of women to confront a powerful enemy instead of submitting in defeat.

Deborah is also a woman, and it is not an oversight or accident that neither the husband of Deborah nor the husband of Jael appear in the story. Jael's husband is identified as Heber the Kennite, but where is he? Deborah is the only woman judge in Israel's history, and her husband is also identified. His name is Lapidot, which means a lightning bolt, but he never enters the story either.

Deborah tells Barak that he will be leading the army of Israel. Barak means the light that flashes across the sky from a bolt of lightning, but Barak responds, "If you will go with me, I will go; but if you will not go with me, I will not go" (Jdg 4:8). As one last comment on the symbolism of names in this story, Deborah means "a bee," which is a tiny insect that can cause a mighty sting.

The symbolism of women filling the roles expected of men in the story of Deborah was apparently composed in the early years of the monarchy when David (or possibly Solomon) needed to unite the twelve tribes under one king.

Why, we ask, is symbolism so prevalent in the biblical text? Let me answer with another question. How did the people of Israel try to explain God, and how did God explain Himself in His Word? After all, no one has seen God at any time (Is 64:4; John 1:18). Furthermore, we learn that God is Spirit (John 4:24), and Spirit is an abstract concept that we cannot see.

You learned in the last session that רוח is a word used for God, and is often translated Spirit. However, רוח can also mean wind or breath. Therefore, wind and breath become symbols to help us understand the abstract nature of God. We cannot see

God, or even grasp His nature in our minds, but we can "experience" Him through symbolism. God is just like wind, which we cannot see, but we can see clouds that have been formed by water vapor, and wind causes them to drift across the sky. It is not the wind we are seeing, but the clouds that the wind is blowing. Then there are dust particles in the air that we feel against our skin when the wind blows. It is not the wind we are feeling, but the dust particles that the wind is blowing. A symbol uses a material object (clouds and dust particles that the wind blows) to represent the abstract nature of God.

Images and Symbols Together

Imagery and symbolism are often used together. Take, for example, the Song of Deborah that we just read. You certainly appreciated the graphic imagery, but what about the symbols? How is Jael a symbol, and what does she represent? Jael, a woman, was the one who killed the enemy, and her weapons were women's tools, a tent peg and a hammer.

As I mentioned earlier, scholars think that chapter 4 of Judges was composed at the time of the United Monarchy in order to bring the twelve tribes together under one king. After all, they had been ruling their individual tribal areas ever since entering the Promised Land after the Exodus, and now they had to submit to a unified ruling power. What better way to convince them to come together to fight a common enemy under the leadership of a king than to spread a story about women as the victorious warriors.

Metaphor

A metaphor is an extended symbol. That is, when one thing represents another (which is a symbol), the relationship between the two has no literal connection. Thus, it becomes a metaphor.

Take, for example, "A mighty fortress is our God." God is likened to a mighty fortress. The image of a powerful walled city, protected by thick and high stone walls, has no literal relationship to God. Yet, we understand the non-literal, metaphorical meaning. Our God is very powerful, and He can protect us with His might. The symbolism has become a metaphor by extending the symbol beyond a literal likeness. God is not literally a walled fortress, but this non-literal symbolism conveys a powerful meaning.

Metaphors are used extensively in Scripture to convey a significant depth of meaning. They can be hard to see because they tend to be subtle and even obscure. We are not supposed to read the passage literally, but to perceive the metaphor and its extended meaning.

Once you learn how to recognize metaphors, you will have no trouble understanding the deeper meaning they convey. The challenge is to identify it as a metaphor. Let me give you a hint. Start by looking for the symbol where one thing stands for something else. "A mighty fortress is our God" uses one thing (a fortress) to represent another (God). However, this is not a simple symbol that offers a quick and easy and literal connection. Identifying God with a mighty fortress forces us to stop and ponder the relationship. So you ask, "How is God a mighty fortress?" This is a metaphor that is leading you to a deeper understanding of God.

What have we just done? First, we saw the symbol. God is represented by a mighty fortress. Then we stopped and spent time asking a question that led to a deeper understanding. *How* is God a mighty fortress? The symbol becomes a metaphor by the extended, non-literal relationship.

Let us practice now with some poetic passages.

> My people have committed two evils:
>> They have forsaken Me,
>> The fountain of living waters,
>
>> To hew for themselves cisterns,
>> Broken cisterns that can hold no water.
>>> Jer 2:13

The first major sin in this verse is forsaking God. The magnitude of the sin is emphasized by the nature of what the people have forsaken.

- In the first sin, what is the symbol? That is, how is one thing representing another?
- How is the symbol extended by a non-literal relationship? That is, how has the symbol become a metaphor?

- The metaphor could have likened God to a fountain of water, but instead it gives us a fountain of living water. How does the image of living water affect the meaning?
- From this metaphor, how would you describe the nature of God?

We are ready now to look at the second major sin, which will explain *how* God's people have forsaken Him.

A cistern in ancient Israel was carved out of rock to capture and hold rain that fell during the rainy season. Rain fell during the six months of winter, and the following dry season lasted for six months in the summer. The cistern had a cover, typically made of wood, which could easily be removed and served to prevent evaporation. The people of Israel depended on God to deliver enough rain in the winter to last them through the dry season. They would carefully store this water in cisterns.

Now it is time for you to carefully examine the metaphor to help you understand human nature that separates God's people from Him.

- Read once more the poetic passage about cisterns. Read for rhythm and emotion in Jeremiah 2:13.
- Now visualize a broken cistern. What is happening?
- Next identify the symbol by completing the sentence, "A broken cistern is _____."
- What does each of these two cisterns represent? One is broken and the other is not.
- The broken cistern that leaks is a contrast to a well built and carefully maintained cistern.
- This metaphor is a hard one to identify because it is obscure. What does God give His children that makes Him known and instructs them how to draw near to Him?
- How can the Word of God be likened to a leaky cistern? Now do you understand what the cistern represents?
- How is the symbol extended by a non-literal relationship? That is, how has the symbol become a metaphor?
- From this metaphor, how would you describe the sin of God's people?

Imagery, Symbolism and Metaphor | **73**

- How does this sin appear in your life as well?

You need to practice identifying and penetrating the meaning of metaphors until it becomes second nature for you to perceive them. So, let us consider one more metaphor, but this time you will be doing all of the work. Start by reviewing in your mind just what it means that a metaphor is an "extended symbol."

- What is a symbol?
- How is a metaphor an extended symbol?
- What is the difference between a symbol and a metaphor?

Now consider a verse in Isaiah, who is talking about "a shoot that will spring from the stem of Jesse." This "shoot" is prophetic of the coming Messiah. Isaiah then goes on to describe the time of judgment, which is still future. Listen carefully, and see if you can identify the metaphor.

He will strike the earth with the rod of his mouth.
Is 11:4

- Start by identifying the symbol, which is one word that represents another.
- How has the symbol been extended to become a metaphor?
- Are you curious about a key word? What is this key word, and why was your curiosity drawn to it?
- It is essential that you use the online concordance to look up the Hebrew word, and the various ways in which this word is used.
- How many times does שבט (*shevet*) appear in the Hebrew Scriptures?
- Where and how is שבט first used? Be sure to read this verse in its context, which is an extraordinary prophetic passage.
- Where and how does שבט – staff/scepter - appear in the second and third occurrences? Again, always read a verse in its context.
- Now you will see in the fourth appearance how שֵׁבֶט is used in Isaiah 11:4. Explain its meaning in this fourth appearance in Genesis.

- Now you are ready to return to Isaiah 11:4. How do all three meanings that you have uncovered from your word study of שבט apply to Isaiah's words about the coming judgment that will be administered by the Messiah?

Conclusion

We are working to recover first century methods of searching the Scriptures, which have the potential to reveal "all answers to life and godliness" as we read in 2 Peter 1:3. The people in ancient Israel believed that God had given them, through His inspired Word, everything they would ever need to know. However, much of that knowledge and understanding is in the depth of Scripture. Those with a heart to know God and to grow close to Him can uncover this deeper meaning, which the New Testament parables call the mysteries of the Kingdom of God (Mat 13:11).

You are learning to uncover these mysteries and to penetrate a depth of understanding in Scripture. To do this, you must listen for vivid imagery and provoking symbols. Most important, you must learn to recognize metaphorical language in Scripture, and then stop to ponder the meaning that these metaphors evoke.

Chapter Six
Symbolism of Names and Numbers

I was taught to read everything in the Bible as a literal record of historical events, which is often the evangelical tradition of Bible study but has also become quite popular among many Christian denominations today. However, the more I became immersed in first century methods of Bible study, the more I realized how "non-literal" the Bible actually is. That does not mean that the events never happened. I believe they did. But the stories are told with such exquisite artistry of language that we are drawn to an ever deeper understanding of our God, our relationship with Him, and the role He is asking us to play.

Let me explain how this literal interpretation became prevalent in Christian tradition. The earliest Christians were Jews. But after the destruction of the temple in 70 A.D., the Romans dispersed the Jews throughout the Roman Empire as a penalty for their revolt against Rome. Christianity then developed with non-Jewish leaders whose way of thinking was Greek, not Hebrew. By the time of the fourth century, Christianity had spread throughout the Roman Empire with members who, for the most part, were not Jews but Gentiles. Furthermore, there was no unified theology, only numerous Christian sects and doctrines.

The Roman emperor Constantine (reigned from 306 to 337) had a major impact on the development of Christianity by bringing together the leading Christian bishops, and requiring them to agree on a unified theology. Two decisions had a major impact on Christianity as we know it today.

First was the debate on whether or not to keep the Hebrew Scriptures in the Christian Bible. After all, the God of Israel seemed different from the God of love and grace in what became the New Testament. The result was a compromise. Keep the Hebrew Scriptures, but call them the "Old" Testament in contrast to the "New" Testament. The New Testament, they believed, conveyed the "true" gospel from God, and the Old Testament was merely a foundation to understand God's new and true revelation of His son, the Messiah.

Second, because the Old Testament was considered merely a foundational understanding for the gospel of Christ, the order of the books in the Hebrew Bible was changed. Instead of a tripartite division of the Torah (first five books of Moses), the Prophets, and the Writings, which was the order of books at the time of Yeshua (and is still the order of the Jewish Bible today), the books were rearranged. Their order became an historical overview of the history of ancient Israel. This historical perspective of the Christian Old Testament is still prevalent today among those who view the Hebrew Scriptures as primarily a literal narrative of ancient Israel.

There is one other momentous event in the history of Christian theology that promoted a literal interpretation of the Bible. During the Protestant Reformation, Martin Luther promoted a new idea about how to perceive and study the Bible. Rather than relying on an exclusive interpretation by priests, because they were the only educated class during the Dark Ages, Luther cried *sola literalis*, meaning only the literal meaning. That is, the educated middle class could now read the Bible for themselves. They did not need to rely on interpretation by others. All they had to do was read the Bible to understand it. Just read the literal meaning, Luther insisted.

Both Literal *and* Depth of Meaning

Returning to the culture of first century Israel, and viewing the Holy Writings as people at the time of Yeshua would have perceived them, has allowed me to understand the Hebraic approach. With a Hebraic perspective there is *both* a literal meaning *and* a deeper aspect of meaning in Scripture. God has placed both in His Word, so both are important.

In Hebrew, the word for "literal" is *p'shat*. The word that conveys the deeper meaning is *midrash*. Let me spend a moment to explain midrash.

The word *midrash* comes from the verbal root *darash* (דרש), which means to seek, study or inquire. There are two forms of midrash in the Jewish tradition. Haggadic midrash retells the biblical narrative in a creative and artistic way that reveals a depth of meaning. This study will not explore haggadic midrash. However, if you would like to learn more, I have two suggestions. First, the Passover Haggadah is read by Jews each year during the

Passover seder, which is a re-telling of the Exodus story.[3] Second, I have come to the conclusion that all the New Testament parables are a form of haggadic midrash, and I have written a book entitled *Uncovering Mysteries in the Parables with Haggadic Midrash*.[4]

The other form of midrash is known as halachic midrash, which uses rabbinic principles to uncover previously hidden meaning from the depth of Scripture. Again, this study will not address halachic midrash. If you wish to learn more I suggest my study of Paul's letter to the Galatians, *The Law is not a Curse: Paul's Midrash in Galatians*.[5]

You may be asking why I even mentioned *midrash*. I simply want to help you understand the Hebraic approach to understanding the Holy Writings. God is the author, who has given both a plain and simple meaning (the literal meaning known as the *p'shat*), and a deeper meaning known as midrash.

There is, however, a third principle that we have been learning, which helps us uncover a depth of understanding in the same way that the common people in ancient Israel would have searched the Scriptures to uncover its hidden meaning. The biblical language itself is filled with artistic nuances and mysterious elements that offer clues to draw us to a depth of meaning with a growing curiosity and a desire to draw closer to God. This is the skill you are learning in this study.

One excellent way to practice perceiving this depth of God's Word is through the symbolism of names and numbers, which we will now address.

Symbolism of Names in Scripture

Not all names in Scripture are symbolic, but many of them are. Perhaps the uncertainty of the symbolism is part of the intrigue.

---

[3] You can find the Passover Haggadah online. Simply Google "Passover Haggadah."

[4] Anne Kimball Davis, *Uncovering Mysteries of the Parables with Haggadic Midrash* (BibleInteract, 2013).

[5] Anne Kimball Davis, *The Law is not a Curse: Paul's Midrash in Galatians* (BibleInteract, 2012). See chapters 5 and 6, pp. 93-145.

Also, God changes the names of two of the patriarchs, Abram to Abraham and Jacob to Israel, which further stimulates our curiosity.

We will begin with Abram, whose name God changed to Abraham, because the Genesis account draws our attention to the meaning of the new name. "No longer shall your name be called Abram," God declared, "but your name shall be Abraham." God then goes on to explain the reason for the new name. "For I will make you the father of a multitude of nations" (Gen 17:5).

Abram means "exalted father." *Av* is father, and *ram* means lifted or exalted. This is certainly a prestigious name, which characterizes the man who obeyed God by leaving behind the known, civilized world of Ur in Babylon to "go to a land that I will show you." However, we are most interested in the new name, Abraham, its meaning and the reason for the change.

The new name Abraham is defined in the biblical passage as meaning "father of a multitude of nations." Let us look at the Hebrew, which is read from right to left.

אב־המון גוים (*av-hamon goyim*)

You recognize *av* as "father." *Hamon* means "many," and *goyim* refers to people who are not Jews. *Goyim* is typically translated "nations." Thus, Abraham's new name prophecies that he will become the father of a large number of people. We certainly see at least a partial fulfillment of that prophecy in the children of Israel. The Apostle Paul explains another in Galatians 3:6-9. Gentiles, who are non-Jewish *goyim*, are becoming children of God by their faith in God's son, Yeshua.

However, you will not be surprised to learn that we can understand more about the meaning of Abraham's new name if we penetrate the linguistic artistry of Genesis 17:5 in its context of verses 1-5. Note that these verses are in the rhythm of Hebrew poetry, so there will be parallel lines with intriguing relationships.

> Now when Abram was ninety-nine years old, the
> Lord appeared to Abram and said to him,
>
> A^1. I am God Almighty;
>   B. Walk before Me,
>   B. and be blameless.

A^2. I will establish My covenant between Me and you,
> B. And I will multiply you exceedingly."

Abram fell on his face, and God talked with him, saying,
A^3. As for Me, behold, My covenant is with you,
> B^1. And you will be the father of a multitude of nations.
>> C^1. No longer shall your name be called Abram, but your name shall be Abraham.
> B^2. For I will make you the father of a multitude of nations.
>> C^2. I will make you exceedingly fruitful
>> C^3. And I will make nations of you
>> C^4. And kings shall come forth from you.

A^4. And I will establish My covenant between Me and you and your descendants after you throughout their generations.   Gen 17:1-7

I have shared with you my perception of the artistic structure that reveals relationships leading to deeper meaning. Start with the A lines. A^2 A^3 A^4 are all about God's covenant. A^1 has a connection to the other A lines because God has the authority to unilaterally declare a covenant relationship with Abraham and his descendants.

As we continue to ponder the relationships between these parallel lines, we see that B^1 and B^2 are parallel by repetition. They are pointing to what is between them and what follows, which are the C lines. C^2, C^3 and C^4 expand and explain the prophetic result of C^1. As the passage continues we read:

> This is My covenant, which you shall keep, between Me and you and your descendants after you: every male among you shall be circumcised.
> And you shall be circumcised in the flesh of your foreskin, and it shall be the sign of the covenant between Me and you. Gen 17:10-11

I suggest that circumcision is not a condition of the covenant but a sign of the covenant (Gen 17:11). If circumcision were a condition, it would be a bilateral agreement where two parties have to agree to establish and honor the covenant agreement. However, I perceive the covenant as unilateral. That is, God has established a covenant relationship with Abraham and his descendants, and has commanded that circumcision be the sign of that covenant.

In our study to understand the meaning of Abraham's new name, we are especially drawn to *why* God changed his name. To uncover this depth of meaning we will turn to the first part of the passage where God begins speaking to Abram (his name at that time). Notice how I have indented God's two directives: "walk before me" and "be blameless." Apparently a "blameless" condition is required in order to "walk before God." The third B line (God will multiply Abram) is the result of being blameless and walking before God.

Let us turn our attention first to the word "blameless." To answer the questions below, you should practice using the interlinear Bible and concordance offered online by biblehub.com.

- What is the Hebrew word for "blameless" in Genesis 17:1?
- How many times does this Hebrew word appear in Scripture?
- Where is the Hebrew word first used, and who is the first person in Scripture who is identified as blameless?
- Returning to the concordance in biblehub.com, what is the second appearance of the word that has been translated "blameless"?
- How is the word used in its third appearance?

The English translation in Genesis 17:1 is "blameless" (NASB). The King James Version has translated "perfect." The word is תמים (*tamim*), which carries the connotation of perfection, that is, without sin or blemish. "Sin" refers to people, and "blemish" applies to animals. I trust you have already discovered the third usage of the word in Exodus 12:1, which explains that animals given to God as a sacrifice had to be תמים, that is, without blemish.

But what does it mean that God instructed Abraham to walk before Him and be תמים? Is it possible for God's people to be

תמים? Is it possible for you to be תמים? We need to return to the story of Noah, where תמים first appears, in order to uncover our answer.

    A. Noah was a righteous man,
    A. Blameless in his time;
        B. Noah walked with God. Gen 6:9

Let me explain the relationships that I see. The first two lines seem to be in a parallel construction. Both "righteous" and "blameless" mean to be in a condition without sin, which is required to come into the presence of God. I placed "Noah walked with God" to the right because I see that as the result of the two parallel A lines. Those who are walking in righteousness will be walking with God. Thus, "blameless" means to be righteous, and those who are righteous will be walking with God.

People who read the Bible literally, and who do not know how to uncover its depth of meaning, often conclude that Noah, and perhaps also Abraham and a few other towering figures in the Bible, may have been righteous. But who are we to think that we can be righteous? For example, if you are reading Genesis 17:1 about Abraham with the echo of Noah in your mind, you must also reflect on other aspects of Noah's character. Noah sinned when he "drank of the wine and became drunk, and uncovered himself inside his tent" (Gen 9:21). "Uncovered himself" is a metaphor for taking off clothing and becoming naked, which becomes a symbol of nakedness that represents a sinful condition. You will remember that God had to "cover" Adam and Eve with the skin of animals. (Perhaps these were unblemished animals given in sacrifice.) We read, "The Lord God made garments of skin for Adam and his wife, and clothed them" (Gen 3:21). That is, God covered their sin. This gracious act of God came immediately after the fall of Adam and Eve in the garden.

The conclusion I have drawn from my continuing study of Scripture is that "righteousness" does not mean completely without sin. Even Noah and Abraham and Jacob and David sinned. Take, for example, David's sins with Bathsheba. First he committed adultery, and then he caused the death of Bathsheba's husband, Uriah. Can there be more grievous sins that these? Yet, David repented, and God withdrew the penalty of death for the murder of Uriah, but did not withhold the consequences for adultery. The child conceived from this adulterous relationship died (2 Sam 12:14).

We can see from the biblical text that God saw David as righteous (2 Sam 22:21-27). So, as I searched the Scriptures to understand what it means to be righteous in God's eyes, I can simply share with you my conclusion, that God only sees the heart. God saw Noah as righteous and תמים, and God saw Abraham as תמים even though their lives were not perfect. God told Noah to walk "with" Him, and God instructed Abraham to "walk before Me."

I suggest that God changed Abram's name because He saw him as righteous. The point I wish to make is that תמים, meaning unblemished and without sin, can be identified with righteousness. However, when God encourages His children to "walk in righteousness," He does not expect complete perfection one-hundred percent of the time. Fortunately God only sees the heart.

As for God's prophetic words, that He will make Abraham a "multitude of nations," I believe this is connected to God's expanding promises to Abraham that include many descendants who will have the power of righteousness to conquer the land by defeating the enemy. This is a huge topic that we will not explore here. I will merely give you one verse that conveys this expanding prophecy.

> I will greatly bless you,
>   I will greatly multiply your seed
>   as the stars of the heavens,
>   as the sand which is on the seashore;
>   And your seed shall possess the gate of their enemies. Gen 22:17

A key phrase in this verse, as it relates to our study of a righteous walk with God, is "possess the gate of their enemies." The gate was the weakest part of a walled city and represents the vulnerability of God's enemy (and our enemy). Those who are prepared to overcome the enemy must be righteous by their humble obedience and trust in God.

Symbolism of Numbers in Scripture

The history of ancient Israel begins with the patriarchs. Then comes bondage in Egypt that ends with the Exodus and forty years of wilderness wandering. The next period in Israel's history is recorded in the Book of Judges when the twelve tribes entered the Promised Land and settled in separate tribal areas.

We can identify with what follows because it can easily happen to each of us. After the death of Joshua, and of all those who had left Egypt and experienced the wilderness wandering, "there arose after them a generation that did not know the Lord, nor yet the work which He had done for Israel" (Jdg 2:10).

How quickly we forget the agonizing trials and tribulations of our forefathers. Can you identify with those who fought in the two world wars, or experienced the holocaust in Germany, or lived through the great depression? We become complacent in our lives, and are caught up with worldly concerns and advantages.

You will remember that "testing" is a form of instruction. God allows us to walk in worldly ways because they generate unpleasant consequences. If we respond to the testing in a proper manner, we learn to leave behind a worldly life and grow in our righteous walk with God.

Returning to the Book of Judges, we see that the children of Israel repeatedly "did evil in the sight of the Lord" (Jdg 2:11; 3:7; 12:2; 4:1; 6:1 10:6; 13:1). Of course, we all sin from time to time, so we must not condemn these early Israelites but identify with them. Listen to what was happening.

> They forsook the Lord, the God of their fathers, who had brought them out of the land of Egypt, and followed other gods from *among* the gods of the peoples who were around them, and bowed themselves down to them; thus they provoked the Lord to anger.
> So they forsook the Lord and served Baal and the Ashtaroth. Jdg 2:12-13

When do we forsake our God? When we think or act in worldly ways. When do we follow other gods? When we place importance on anything that is worldly, such as money, possessions, the excitement of power, or the lust of desires.

God was teaching His people how to leave the ways of the world and turn to Him through a continuing process of testing. Listen again to the narrative.

> A. The anger of the Lord burned against Israel,
> > B. And He gave them into the hands of plunderers who plundered them;
> > B. And He sold them into the hands of their enemies around *them*,
> A. So that they could no longer stand before their enemies. Jdg 2:14

Consider the ABBA construction that I heard. God's people allowed themselves to return to the slavery of the world, which is conveyed by literal bondage from surrounding enemy tribes who controlled them for the purpose of exploitation. However, each time God's anger allowed the enemy to conquer, control and devastate, "the sons of Israel cried to the Lord" whereupon God would "raise up a judge to lead them in His ways" (Jdg 3:9, 15; 4:3; 6:6).

> A. When the Lord raised up judges for them,
> > B. the Lord was with the judge
> > B. and delivered them from the hand of their enemies all the days of the judge;
> A. for the Lord was moved to pity by their groaning because of those who oppressed and afflicted. Jdg 2:18

We hear the echo of the Exodus when God heard their "groaning" from the oppression of slavery (cf. Ex 2:24). We hear the prophecy of God's Messiah, who will lead the people in righteousness and judge them when they are unrighteous. However, the focus of this study is on what follows God's deliverance when His people turned to Him. We see in the Book of Judges a cycle of "rest" each time God delivered His people. The "rest" signifies peace from the enemy and a condition of alignment and harmony with God.

Symbolism of Names and Numbers | 85

The Book of Judges repeats this cycle of falling back to the ways of the world, crying out to the Lord, and the Lord delivering them through a judge. What especially catches our attention is the exact number forty that is the period of rest between the cycles. Carefully read these verses, and ponder the questions that follow.

> After Othniel delivered the people, "the land had rest forty years." Jdg 3:11

> After Deborah led Barak to deliver the people, "the land was undisturbed for forty years." Jdg 5:31

> After Gideon delivered the people, "the land was undisturbed for forty years." Jdg 8:28

> "Now the sons of Israel again did evil in the sight of the Lord, so that the Lord gave them into the hands of the Philistines forty years." Jdg 13:1

- In the first three verses, what is the nature of the repetition that you hear?
- In the first three verses, what are the key words?
- How are the first three verses similar?
- Did you hear something in the fourth verse that was startling and different? Explain.

The first three periods of forty years follow a victory over the enemy, which leads to peace that is a quiet time without oppression. But look again at the fourth verse where there is oppression by the Philistines for forty years because the people are doing evil in the sight of the Lord. The ancient Israelites would have been startled by this sudden shift. They would have been asking, "Why is the number forty repeated, and what does it mean?" They would especially have been drawn to another question. "Why does God suddenly shift from forty years of rest to forty years of oppression?"

An indispensable source for finding the symbolic meaning of numbers in the Bible is online and free to the public. The book is *Number in Scripture* by E. W. Bullinger (originally published in 1894). I have found the most useful online source for this reference to be hosted by levendwater.org. I suggest you google "Bullinger Number in Scripture" and select the Levendwater site, which contains an index that will take you directly to the number you are seeking.

- Find Bullinger's *Number in Scripture* on the Levendwater website.
- Scroll down and click on the number forty.
- Does the number forty appear frequently or infrequently in Scripture?
- What does the number forty represent?
- What is the relationship between the number forty and the number nine?
- Of the fifteen periods of forty years in Scripture, Bullinger has placed them into five categories. What are the five categories, and what is an example in Scripture for each of the five categories?

By looking up the number forty in Bullinger, you discovered that it signifies a period of probation, trial and chastisement. It is important to note that the number forty does not signify judgment, but instruction and training. Take, for example, the forty years of wilderness wandering after the Exodus from Egypt. God gave His children the Law to instruct them how to walk in His ways, and used a process of testing to help them learn by experience. The purpose of these forty years of wilderness experience was to prepare the Israelites to enter the Promised Land in order to defeat the enemy and claim their inheritance. However, not all were able to enter. God made a selection of those who were properly trained and prepared.

Now it is time for you to ponder the repetitive period of forty years in the Book of Judges.

- A period of rest followed victory. How was the victory won, and how was rest a blessing?
- What do you think is the significance of the following forty years of rest that followed a victory? What always followed the forty years of rest?

- What do you think was the purpose of the forty years of rest?
- The last period of forty years was not rest after a victory, but domination by the enemy that required God's help. What do you think is the meaning of this forty years of trial and tribulation?
- Why do you think there were three accounts of forty years of rest following a victory? (Consider the symbolism of the number three.)
- Why do you think there was just one account, at the end of the Book of Judges, of forty years of trial and tribulation? (Consider this symbolism of the number one.)

Before concluding, I think it is important to apply the imagery of the number forty in the Book of Judges to our lives today. In this process of application, we will echo the story of Noah, who walked *with* God, and Abraham, who walked *before* God.

Certainly all of us face the enemy of the world, an enemy which entices us with material wealth, a sense of security, and what we have come to call "happiness." We become complacent until something happens to cause pain and suffering. Only then do we typically cry out to the Lord. Yet, our cry for help is meaningless until, and unless, we are led by, follow, and obey the "judge" whom God has sent (His son and our Messiah Yeshua). The "rest" that follows, when we experience peace and harmony with God, allows us to be like Noah who was righteous and blameless (תמים). Noah walked with God.

Are you surprised to learn that this wonderful walk with God is not the final "rest" in our lives today? After experiencing rest and walking with God we begin to grow in our service to God under the leadership of our Lord and master Yeshua. There is work to be done, and God is calling us to be servants who will participate in His great plan of redemption that will ultimately bring all of His children to Him in righteousness. As servants, we willingly leave the peace of "rest" and return to face the enemy. Our battle is spiritual. As we learn to walk *with* God in righteousness, we must "put on the full armor of God so that we will be able to stand firm against the schemes of the devil"

(Eph 6:11). Then comes a second stage in our walk with God. We become leaders of God's people by witnessing the walk of the kingdom, and we become like Abraham who walked *before* God, which the early Jewish sages suggested was walking as a leader before the people of God. "Walk before me and be perfect [תמים]," God told Abraham when He changed Abram's name to Abraham, signifying that he was worthy of this leadership role.

Chapter Seven
Echoes and Commentary

We have spent the first six sessions working in the Hebrew Scriptures with Hebrew words. This approach has helped you learn how to use ancient methods of Bible study as follows:

1. At the time of the gospel events, the New Testament had not yet been written. The Holy Writings for Yeshua and the early Christians were the Hebrew Scriptures.
2. People in first century Israel made God the center of their lives. They turned to the Hebrew Scriptures to help direct their actions.
3. There were no written Bibles in the homes. Typically, in the synagogue there would have been one scroll of the Torah, and perhaps one or more other scrolls. So, in the ancient culture of Israel children learned by memorization beginning in the home. Boys would continue their education in the synagogue where they would learn to read from a Torah scroll and perhaps from other synagogue scrolls like Isaiah and the Psalms. However, instruction was delivered orally and learning continued to be largely by memorization.
4. People believed that God had placed everything in the Holy Writings they would ever need to know. If information was not in the plain and simple meaning (the *p'shat*), then God had embedded what they needed in the depth of Scripture (*midrash*). These hidden mysteries could be uncovered by those with a heart to grow close to God.
5. All the Jews were God's children because God called them His firstborn son and He was their Father. God encouraged them to walk in righteous ways by obeying the Law, and by learning through experiences called "testing."
6. The purpose of righteousness, which was the goal of learning the Law, was to draw near to God. Coming close to the Heavenly Father could only be accomplished by changing from worldly behavior to a righteous manner of living.

With this background information, you will not be surprised to learn that there are over 300 citations in the New Testament from the Hebrew Scriptures. Stop for a moment and consider the reasons why.

Until fairly recently Bible scholars viewed most of these citations as proof texts. That is, they believed that the first Christians saw many prophecies in the Hebrew Scriptures being fulfilled by Yeshua of Nazareth, which explains the abundance of citations in the New Testament. Take, for example, Yeshua who was born in Nazareth where he would have been expected to live and follow in the footsteps of his father. However, Yeshua left Nazareth and settled in Capernaum. Then we read, "This [settling in Capernaum] was to fulfill what was spoken through the prophet Isaiah" (Mat 4:13-16). In the following quotation Isaiah declares that "those people who were sitting in darkness saw a great light" (Mat 4:16 citing Is 9:2). Where were these people who saw a great light? Isaiah tells us they were "in the land of Zebulun and the land of Naphtali." How well do you know your geography? These two tribes of Zebulun and Naphtali settled in the hills of Upper Galilee where Nazareth is located. Capernaum is also in the Galilee but in the portion called the Lower Galilee.

Now we can return to Matthew, who was citing from Isaiah as a proof text. This great light appeared "by the way of the sea beyond the Jordan, Galilee of the Gentiles." The trade route was known as the "way of the sea," and it passed through Capernaum. "Beyond the Jordan, Galilee of the Gentiles" refers to the area on the other side of the Sea of Galilee from Capernaum where two Roman Decapolis cities were inhabited largely by Gentiles. Yeshua spent time during his ministry going to "the other side," which was the Gentile area. Thus, the life and ministry of Yeshua was "proving" these prophetic passages from Isaiah, and Matthew had crafted a proof text.

However, viewing all or most of the 300+ citations in the New Testament as proof texts often leaves the interpretation unclear or unsatisfying. Therefore, scholars have continued to explore the reason that New Testament authors cited the Hebrew Scriptures so frequently.

In 1976-7 two academic works were published, each with a similar revolutionary message that rocked the traditional understanding of most New Testament scholars. Krister Stendahl introduced the idea that Paul was a Jew whose thought and writings are Hebraic. E. P. Sanders investigated areas of Jewish thought in the writings of Paul.[6]

When I first ordered Stendahl's book through the interlibrary loan system, it arrived with ink notations that had been written there by a previous reader. Most disturbing was a swastika symbol whose message was clear. Stendahl was suggesting something contrary to general Christian beliefs, and therefore his proposal was, to some, an evil threat to mainline Christianity.

Stendahl and Sanders precipitated a slow but growing response to their suggestion about the Hebraic nature of the New Testament. Most notable has been the work of James D. G. Dunn, a prolific scholar and author who has greatly advanced our knowledge.[7]

Then in 1993 a work by Richard Hayes had a major impact. In his ground-breaking book, *Echoes of Scripture in the Letters of Paul*, Hays perceived Paul as a Jew who knew the Hebrew Scriptures intimately, and who relied on them as the foundation of his writings. Hays then suggested that Paul was using not only direct citations but also allusions that he called "echoes." These subtle references to the Hebrew Scriptures would have prompted the larger narrative or passage in the minds of those who had memorized the Scriptures. Thus, many of the citations were not merely proof texts, but were carefully crafted methods of interpretation that used pieces of a citation which would have stimulated the larger passage. Furthermore, subtle changes in the citation were apparently intended to convey a commentary with incisive meaning.[8]

---

[6] Krister Stendahl, *Paul among Jews and Gentiles* (Minneapolis: Fortress Press, 1976). E. P. Sanders, *Paul and Palestinian Judaism* (Minneapolis: Fortress Press, 1977).

[7] James D. G. Dunn, *The New Perspective on Paul* (Eerdmans, 2007).

[8] Richard Hayes, *Echoes of Scripture in the Letters of Paul* (Yale, 1993). This book is a collection of earlier essays.

Much work has been done since these influential publications, and my work to recover ancient methods of Bible study is in the mainstream of this linguistic-critical approach.

In this session you will practice listening for "echoes" in the New Testament that refer to narratives and passages in the Hebrew Scriptures. Therefore, it is important that you first master the Greek alphabet so you can work with Greek New Testament words. (You will find a video for learning the Greek alphabet at bibleinteract.com.) However, with all these echoes you will be returning to the Hebrew Scriptures frequently since the New Testament echoes are pointing to Old Testament passages.

Practice Using Ancient Methods

I was once asked by a group of Christians, who were committed to studying the Hebrew Scriptures and were appropriating these messages into their lives, how to respond to the criticism that they were "putting themselves back under the law" by studying the Old Testament. Apparently their accusers perceived the Hebrew Scriptures as "the law," and they believed that Jesus had "done away with the law." Thus, they saw little value in studying the Old Testament except as it foretold the coming of Jesus the Messiah.

As I started to search the Scriptures for an answer, I decided to begin with Paul's words to the Romans. "You are not under law, but under grace" (Rom 6:14b). I will share with you how I used ancient methods to uncover this mystery that penetrates an exciting depth of meaning. I will be using the Hebraic approach of prompting you to ponder the questions. I will do this by asking questions and then giving you time to conduct your own search before I share my thoughts.

- Start by identifying the immediate context of Romans 6:14b. Where does the immediate context begin and where does it end?
- What is the main idea of the immediate context?
- Besides the immediate context, there is also a larger context. What do you think is the larger context? (Hint: there is not a right or wrong answer; draw your own conclusion and be prepared to explain it to your study partner or group).

- What is the main idea of the larger general context?
- How does Romans 6:14b fit into the general context?

Now it is time to examine the linguistic details of the context. Read Romans 6:1-10, and take note that these verses appear in a kind of list. Explain in your own words what each verb is conveying, and take time to carefully ponder the meaning before considering the list that follows.

- Died (to sin)
- Baptized (into the death of Christ)
- Buried (with Christ)
- Walk (in newness of life)
- United (in the likeness of his death)
- United (in his resurrection)
- Crucified (the old self)

All this is what Christ has accomplished for us, but the question becomes this. Will we believe it, claim it, and walk in it? Therefore, Paul creates a transition verse before he shifts to incisive exhortation. We will turn now to the transition between Romans 6:1-10 and Romans 6:12-14.

> Consider yourselves to be dead to sin,
> but alive to God in Christ Jesus. Rom 6:11.

In a sense, this verse draws a conclusion to the passage that precedes it. Christ has made you alive with him by his death and resurrection. However, now you must become dead to sin, so the transition also acts as an introduction to what follows. We must desire the life we just encountered in verses 1-10, but to do that we must become "dead to sin." Paul now instructs us how to be dead to sin. "Do not let sin reign over your mortal body that you should obey its lusts" (Rom 6:12).

Note that this is a negative commandment. "Do not" let sin reign over you. When you do, there will be consequences because you will not be obeying God. Instead you will be obeying the "lusts of sin." The negative commandment continues. "Do not go on presenting the members of your body to sin as instruments of unrighteousness."

94 | Recovering Ancient Methods of Bible Study

Suddenly we are confronted with a contrast.

> Therefore do not let sin reign in your mortal body so that you obey its lusts, and do not go on presenting the members of your body to sin as instruments of unrighteousness;
> BUT
> Present yourselves to God as those alive from the dead, and your members as instruments of righteousness to God. For sin shall not be master over you, for you are not under law but under grace. Rom 6:12-13

Did you hear the repetitions?
- Sin (reign and master over)
- Present (yourself)
- Members (of your body)
- Instruments (of righteousness or unrighteousness)
- Under (law or grace)

Our ear has been drawn to the repetition, which is forming parallel lines. Did you hear it? These verses form an ABCBA construction, which you can now construct in the box below.

- What word connects the two A lines? What is the relationship between these two parallel lines?
- What makes the two B lines parallel? What is the relationship between them?
- The two parallel A lines, and the two parallel B lines, are all pointing to the chiastic center C, which should cause you to stop with intense emotion. What does it mean to "present yourself to God as alive from the dead?"

The verse that began this entire study is in the second A line. "You are not under law, but under grace" (Rom 6:14). Now can you see that when we started with "you are not under law, but under grace," we read these words out of their context? Not only must we see the words in their general context, which we have just finished doing, but we must also resist taking only a portion of a verse. The complete verse reads, "Sin shall not be master over you, for you are not under law, but under grace" (Rom 6:14). We will now see that "sin shall not be master over you" is an echo from the Cain and Abel story.

Paul Echoes the Cain and Abel Story

We have already spent time in Session Four working on a key word in the Cain and Abel story. We discovered in Gen 4:1-4 that Abel brought the firstborn of his flock, which was acceptable to God because the firstborn animal and first fruits of produce are the very best one can give. Cain, on the other hand, simply brought an offering, not the first fruit of his produce. Take time now to reread Genesis 4:1-4. Then continue reading Genesis 4:5-7, which is what we will be working on now.

In the verse we are contemplating in Romans 6:14, do you hear how Paul is echoing the story of Cain in Genesis 4:7? Listen for a word or concept that Paul is repeating in such a way that those who had memorized Scripture would have heard the echo.

> PAUL: Sin shall not be master over you, for you are not under law, but under grace. Rom 6:14

> GOD TO CAIN: If you do well, will not *your countenance* be lifted up? And if you do not do well, sin is crouching at the door; and its desire is for you, but you must master it." Gen 4:7

In Genesis, we are encouraged to be a master over sin. In his letter to the Romans, Paul has taken the same concept and turned it into a more forceful negative commandment. We are not to let sin be a master over us. I suggest that the early recipients of Paul's letter would have heard this "echo." After all, they had memorized Scripture, not verse by verse, but in blocks or portions of the Holy Writings.

You too have "heard" this echo because I have just guided you to read the passage. Did you read it slowly and carefully so you could "hear" the echo? So, what must you do next? Try to answer this question first before continuing because there is much work to be done to make meaning of Paul's verse about law and grace. What must you do next?

Hebraic Approach to Learning

In Session One I encouraged you to "think Hebrew, not Greek." You need to practice this skill now.

The Greek approach proceeds with the understanding that mankind can discover the truths of Scripture. Furthermore, our western tradition elevates the teacher because he (or she) knows these truths. Therefore, you may be waiting for me to offer my observations. However, I encourage you to "think Hebrew, not Greek," so carefully consider the questions that follow and answer them to the best of your ability.

- In Genesis 4:4-5, what is the contrast? How does this contrast act as a clue for understanding the passage? What is the message that the contrast conveys? How is the message relevant to your life today?
- How does the last sentence in Genesis 4:5 ("Cain became very angry and his countenance fell") portray a vivid image, and how does this image become the beginning of another unit of thought that continues through Genesis 4:7?

- What repetitions do you hear in verses 5-6? Describe the vivid mental picture stimulated by this repetition.
- "Lifted up" is the English translation of an important Hebrew word. What is the Hebrew word?
- What is the verse where this Hebrew word (translated "lifted up" in the NASB) first appears? How many times is it used in this one verse?
- What is the second verse where this Hebrew word appears? From the context in which it appears in this second verse, what seems to be the meaning? With this meaning in mind, return to the first appearance. What do you think is the meaning there?
- In Gen 4:7, the translators of the NASB have added *countenance* because it is implied. Now read the verse without *countenance*, which is a better translation of the original text. How does this change the meaning? (Hint: the answer to this question is critical to your understanding and the depth of meaning).

If you have conducted the word study prompted by the English translation "lifted up," I trust you have perceived the contrast between "falling" because of sin and being "exalted" by offering yourself to God without sin. ("Lifted up" is the English translation of שאת *se'et* which can also mean "exalted"). I find this message thrilling because God spoke words of instruction to Cain, not condemnation. Cain was a sinner who presented himself to God in an unrighteous condition, and God responded with instruction.

Let me stop for a moment and comment on the relevance of this passage to our lives today. We must consider that the story of Cain and Abel is highly metaphorical. That is, the narrative is stimulating instruction by extending a symbol in a non-literal way to become a metaphor. Cain's failure to offer his best to God symbolically represents the actions of many of God's children. In the New Testament, which expands and comments on the Hebrew Scriptures, we learn that those with faith in Christ are a "kind of first fruits" to God (James 1:18). That is, we are encouraged to give ourselves to God with the very best we have to offer. Paul explains this principal in Romans 12:1 where we learn that we are to be a "living and holy sacrifice" to God, not an offering that is corrupted by sin.

You are now ready to understand the continuing metaphorical instruction in the Cain and Abel story of how sin works in your life. A crouching lion is used as a symbol. "Sin is crouching at the door" alludes to lions that lived in the dense undergrowth of the Jordan River Valley.

- How is "sin crouching at the door" a metaphor?
- How does this metaphor help us understand how sin operates in our lives?

I have chosen to instruct you in the meaning of these three verses by leading you to conduct your own search, and to ponder a depth of meaning in discussion with your peers. As I posed questions for you to consider, you should also practice this skill of asking your own pertinent questions that lead to searching for depth of understanding.

You have already worked the contrast between the offerings of Cain and Abel. Now Paul prompts you to consider "Cain became very angry and his countenance fell." Can you picture Cain's fallen face? This imagery leads to a discussion, not of Cain nor of his fallen face, but to a non-literal concept.

Paul is directing our thoughts in Romans 6:1-14, through the echo of this Cain and Abel story, to the way sin operates in our lives. We have a choice between "doing well," in which case we will be exalted in God's eyes, or not doing well, which will open the door to sin and its consequences. This is the echo that the recipients of Paul's letter would likely have heard from Paul's provocative words, "Sin shall not be master over you, for you are not under law but under grace."

We are now drawn by the repetition and contrast of "under" in "you are no longer under law but under grace." Therefore, we must now take this understanding of how sin operates in our lives back to Paul's letter to the Romans and the repetition of "under."

Under Law or Under Grace

We have been using an ancient approach to searching the Scriptures by listening for anything unusual. In the words of Paul we perceived a contrast and heard an echo from the Cain and Abel story. When we explored the echo we heard a repetition, responded to vivid imagery, identified a key word, and applied the meaning about sin to our lives today. We are now ready to listen again to our original verse. "You are not under law, but under grace." I will pose questions to help you consider this one terse comment.

- What do you think is the contrast between law and grace?
- Do you hear the repetition of "under"?
- Why is the repetition a key word? (Hint: there is more to this answer than repetition).
- What do you do with a key word?

Stop now and explore the meaning of the key word "under." The Greek word that has been translated "under" is the preposition ὑπό, which can convey different nuances of meaning depending on the context.

- Find Romans 6:14 in biblehub.com. How does Strong's concordance explain the three different nuances of the meaning of ὑπό?
- Why have the translators selected "under" as the meaning in the context of this passage?
- Scroll down the list of verses in biblehub.com that use ὑπό. Stop and carefully read the verses that translate ὑπό as "under." List three relevant verses below with brief notes about each one.

- Do you see that most verses translating ὑπό as "under" are using the word for a physical location? Scroll down the concordance list again to consider this observation.
- In Matthew 8:9, can you see that ὑπό appears twice? This verse in Matthew is using ὑπό in a way that is similar to Romans 6:14. What is the sense of meaning in Matthew 8:9?

Did you see in Matthew 8:9 that the Roman centurion not only had command of the soldiers under him, but he was also *under the authority* of those who ruled over him. We can now understand what Paul is trying to tell us with the word ὑπό. We are no longer *under the authority* of the law (meaning laws). Why and when? Those with faith in Christ now have the Holy Spirit to guide them, which was one function of the Law that contained laws, but is now the role of the Holy Spirit. However, Paul gives us a startling word of warning. In order for us to be guided by the Holy Spirit, we must put ourselves *under the authority* of grace, which is the authority of God. How do we put ourselves under His authority? We submit in humble obedience by our love for His son and our faith in him. Only then are we no longer under the authority of the law, but under the authority of grace.

How well do you now understand "you are no longer under law but under grace"?

- What does it mean to submit to the authority of grace?
- Describe someone you know who has submitted to the authority of grace.
- If one submits to the authority of grace, why is there no need for the law?
- How do believers in Christ submit to the authority of grace?
- The term "law" can refer to the Torah, or it can refer to all of the Hebrew Scriptures, in which case I call it the Law (capital "L"). The word "torah" means "instruction," so the term "law" can also refer to specific laws identified in the Hebrew Scriptures.

- Why do you think I have capitalized Law when it refers to the Hebrew Scriptures, and I have not capitalized law when it applies to specific laws?
- Which meaning of "law" do you think Paul is using when he says, "We are no longer under law but under grace?" Explain your answer.
- Why do believers in Christ, who fail to submit to the authority of grace, still need the "law"?
- Paul does not say we have been set free from the law. Instead he says we have been set free from sin (Rom 6:7, 18, 22, 23). Return to Romans and review these verses. Then explain the difference between "set free from the law" and "set free from sin."
- How did Christ come to fulfill the law as we read in Matthew 5:17? (Hint: consider and look up key words).

Another Echo in Hebrews 3:5-6

You will now practice with another echo. You will need to use your new skills of listening to the artistic nuances of the text, and then you will continue to ask questions that will probe for deeper meaning.

> 5 Now ^{a}Moses was faithful in all His house as ^{b}a servant, ^{c}for a testimony of those things ^{d}which were to be spoken later;
> 6 but Christ *was faithful* as ^{a}a Son over His house-- ^{b}whose house we are, ^{c}if we hold fast our ^{d}confidence and the boast of our ^{e}hope firm until the end. Heb 3:5-6

I draw your attention to the small superscript letters that appear in the NASB Reference Edition. This is an important tool for your ability to perceive the Hebraic nature of the New Testament. The superscript letters point to notes in the middle margin, which often list echoes in both the Hebrew Scriptures and the New Testament. I personally find the echoes in the Hebrew Scriptures most helpful because that is what the earliest Christians would have heard.

102 | Recovering Ancient Methods of Bible Study

For you to "hear" and appreciate the echoes in this passage, and to perceive their relationship to our verses in the New Testament Book of Hebrews, you must go back to the Hebrew Scriptures and read these echoes in their context before returning to the New Testament passage. If you do not already have a good reference Bible that lists these echoes, you should consider obtaining one.

For this exercise, I will list the middle margin information. You should take time to read each in its context. Take brief notes below, and then you can return to Hebrews 3:5-6.

Middle Margin	Brief Notes
[a]Ex 40:16; Num 12:7; Heb 3:2	
[b]Ex 14:31; Num 12:7	
[c]Deut 18:18 ff.	
[d]Heb 1:1	

Now it is time for you to practice asking questions that will help you penetrate a depth of meaning. You can start with Hebrews 3:5.

- What questions can you ask about "faithful" and "servant"? How does this information relate to Moses?

- Are you curious about the word "testimony"? Use the online concordance to gain a meaning of the original Greek word.
- Why and how is Deuteronomy 18:18 connected with "testimony"?
- Have you thought about Moses as a prophetic "type" of Christ? What does this mean?

Now you should look at the marginal notes for Hebrews 3:6. How many marginal notes are there? What catches your attention about all six of these marginal notes? Because they all refer to New Testament passages I am not drawn to them, which is why I have not inserted a chart for you to make brief notes. However, do not stop asking yourself questions that probe for deeper meaning.

- Are you curious about the contrast between Heberws 3:5 and Hebrews 3:6?
- What is the main idea of the contrast?
- Are you curious about the nature of the evidence for the contrast? What is the evidence?
- Are you thinking about the relationship between a servant and a son? What is this relationship, and how does it apply to this passage?
- What other questions are you asking?

As for me, I see a common Hebrew perspective that is expressed as "how much more." Thus, how much more is Yeshua, who is the "son" of God, than Moses, who was a faithful "servant" of God? If we think of a household in ancient Israel, a son would have a higher position than a servant.

I also see a contrast between the two houses (which are made up of people). So, how much more is the house of Yeshua (those who have the gift of the Holy Spirit through their faith in Christ) than the house of Moses (those who have only the written law).

Perhaps most important from my perspective is where we, as believers in Christ, fit into this powerful visual image. We are *both* sons of God (by our faith in His son), *and* we can be servants in Yeshua's house *if* we submit in humble obedience. Those who are sons can become servants when they truly live and witness a life that is "how much more." The irony is that the role of a servant has become higher than that of a son.

These are only my thoughts. You may have stimulated your own thoughts by asking questions. In any case, the echoes from the Hebrew text, which are recorded in the middle margin of the NASB, led us to a depth of meaning that is penetrating beyond merely reading the words in the New Testament passage.

Commentary on the Hebrew Scriptures

A commentary accomplishes exactly what the word conveys. It comments on some other portion of a text.

Take, for example, the Torah, which is a collection of five books – Genesis, Exodus, Leviticus, Numbers and Deuteronomy. Originally these were not "books" as we know them in our Bibles today, but individual scrolls. We think these five individual scrolls were collected into one scroll known as the Torah (or Five Books of Moses) during the Babylonian exile.

However, consider the last book, which is Deuteronomy, a name that is a composite of two Greek words meaning "second law." Stop and think for a moment. Why would Deuteronomy be called the *second* law? How well do you know Deuteronomy in order to compare it with the first four books of the Torah? Deuteronomy retells much of what is contained in Exodus, Numbers and Leviticus. Although all five books of the Torah are called the "five books of Moses," scholars now generally suggest that Deuteronomy was composed at a later time, possibly in the 7th century B.C. during the period of religious reform promoted by King Josiah. Thus, Deuteronomy is a commentary on three books of the Torah, which is why it is called the "second law."

We have seen that the order of the books at the time of Yeshua was different from the order in our Bibles today. The Torah (first five books of Moses) comes first in both the Christian and Jewish Bibles. However, the Jewish Bible then follows with a collection called the Prophets, which is followed by another collection called the Writings. The Christian Bible, on the other hand, rearranged the order of the Prophets and the Writings to create an historical background for the New Testament.

Let us consider now the books of the Prophets. If you spend time working diligently in these books, you will discover many echoes from the Torah. In fact, the Prophets are a commentary on the Torah. The reason for this commentary is important in our efforts to return to the way of understanding the Scriptures as the people of ancient Israel would have perceived them. They believed that the Torah was a direct revelation from God to Moses. Therefore, the Torah was viewed as the kernel or core of the Holy Writings. The prophets, although receiving direct communication from God, were commenting on this central portion of God's communication to His people. The same was true with the Writings. They were also considered a commentary on the Torah.

Now we come to the heart of this discussion on commentaries in the Bible. Do you remember that there are over 300 direct citations in the New Testament of the Old Testament, and for every clear citation there are many more echoes or allusions. What, then, does this make the New Testament but a commentary on the Hebrew Scriptures? Certainly there is new information that is available in the light of God's son, the Messiah. However, I cannot emphasize enough this observation of the New Testament as a commentary on the Old. If you incorporate this understanding in your study of the Bible as a guiding principle, you will be transported back to the first century, the time of Yeshua. You will begin to see all of the Holy Writings, both the Old and New Testaments, as one unified message. You will receive the text as it was intended to be heard. You must then take the ancient message and apply it to your own life today. However, I suggest it is important that you first understand the message as it was delivered to the original recipients.

Chapter Eight
Word Study, Patterns, and Sharing Discoveries

You already know how to do a word study. In Session Four you learned how to use the online concordance at www.biblehub.com. Let us review the steps in a word study.

- You will always begin with a word, so you must develop the habit of reading the Scriptures on a regular basis. Then let your curiosity be drawn to a key word.
- I suggest you use biblehub.com for its interlinear Bible. Type in the verse that contains your word and hit enter.
- Find your word in the interlinear verse and speak aloud (literally or in your mind) the Hebrew (Old Testament) or Greek (New Testament) word.
- Above the Hebrew or Greek word you will find Strong's number. Click on that number.
- If you look at Strong's definition in the top left portion of the next page, you must remember that this is an English translation, which is totally inadequate for a depth of understanding your Hebrew or Greek word.
- At the top right of this same page you will see the number of times that the original Hebrew or Greek word appears in Scripture. This is where you want to begin.
- Below the number of occurrences will be a list of the verses that contain the original Hebrew or Greek word. You may need to scroll down to see them all.
- Always start with the first usage. The Jewish sages believed that God placed this word first for a reason, and He marked its meaning in a special way.
- Now make a list of the verses where your Hebrew or Greek word appears. Take brief notes as you read each verse in its context. The context will give you a sense of meaning by the way the word is being used.
- If you are working on a Hebrew word, and there are many occurrences of the word, then you may wish to limit your list to the Torah.

This is as far as I took you in Session Four. In this session you will continue to practice conducting a word study. However, I will now take you to the following two steps, which help you identify one or more patterns that will emerge from your list of details. Then you will learn how to communicate what you have discovered by first presenting the pattern and then supporting what you have learned with biblical evidence.

Are you an Inductive or Deductive Thinker?

Psychologists suggest that all people generally process information predominantly in one of two ways, which they have labeled inductive and deductive. Of course, there are many nuances to this basic principle, but for our purpose we will simply look at the two general categories. The goal of this exercise is for you to decide which of the two best describes your process of thought. If you are an inductive thinker, you will uncover patterns one way. If you are a deductive thinker, you will perceive these patterns in another way.

I am an inductive thinker and, from my experience as a teacher, so are the majority of people. You may or may not be an inductive thinker. So listen carefully to my explanation, and decide if this describes your process of thinking.

I am a person who needs and likes details. As this applies to my practice of reasoning, I am especially impatient with people who argue with general ideas but have no support for their positions. "How did you draw that conclusion," I might ask (perhaps even demand). It often appears to me that they are simply spouting the interpretation of others, which I consider to be improper and perhaps even dangerous. I can't help but think that they have not first considered the evidence nor are they supporting their ideas with details. However, this perception, that they may be relying exclusively or predominantly on the work of others, rather than coming to their own conclusion based on the evidence, may or may not be correct. If the person is a deductive thinker, his or her proposal is worth considering (more on deductive thinking in a moment). However, as an inductive thinker, I start with details and then draw general conclusions. I like my details, and I have to work at perceiving patterns from the details. I sometimes "bog down" my listeners with my excitement of the details I have discovered.

I am in awe of deductive thinkers because they see global patterns without first having to plod through the maze of details. In my experience (and this is only a personal observation) many Jews are deductive thinkers. I find that interesting, and I assume there is some genetic explanation. However, from what I have read, the general population has a much smaller percentage of deductive thinkers than inductive.

So, are you a deductive thinker? If so, you intuitively see general ideas and interpretations, not the interpretation of others but your own perceptions and broad thoughts. Or, are you an inductive thinker who loves the details and has difficulty perceiving global ideas? How you proceed in this chapter, where you will be learning how to uncover patterns in Scripture, will depend on the way you process information.

Start with a List of Details

If you are an inductive thinker, the task of starting with a list of details is relatively easy. The details come from your word study, and you have made a list of the verses in which your word appears in Scripture. You have read each verse in its context, and you have taken brief notes on the verses you think are significant. Your challenge is about to begin. You will need to browse through these details and find one or more patterns. We will work on that in a minute.

If you are a deductive thinker, this task of listing the verses and reading each one in its context will probably be tedious, troublesome, and might even seem irrelevant to your work. However, "have no worries" as they say in Australia. You have already seen the pattern, probably even before you started the word study. Your challenge is not to find a pattern, but to take all the details from your word study and use them to support your global idea. You must also judge from the details whether your general perception is biblical, or perhaps needs some modification based on the detailed evidence you have uncovered from Scripture.

Practice with a Simple Word Study

I have selected a word in the New Testament for you to study for two reasons. First, it only appears four times, so you will be pleased to hear that your list of details will be short. Far more important, the pattern that emerges from these details is provocative with a powerful application to our lives today. You will likely be intrigued by the pattern, and I trust you will learn how to perceive your own patterns by following this example.

We will start, of course, by reading in Scripture and letting our curiosity draw us to a key word. So, we will turn now to a passage where Paul is directing words of instruction to the Romans.

> ¹I urge you, brethren, by the mercies of God, to present your bodies a living and holy <u>sacrifice</u>, acceptable to God, *which is* your spiritual service of <u>worship</u>.
> ² And do not be <u>conformed</u> to this world, but be <u>transformed</u> by the renewing of your mind, so that you may <u>prove</u> what the will of God is, that which is good and acceptable and <u>perfect</u>. Rom 12:1-2

What word (or words) captures your attention? Where does your curiosity lead you? There are several possibilities that I have underlined. This passage is rich, and studying it could occupy you for hours, perhaps even days.

Stop now and consider the key words. Where does your curiosity take you - to one word in particular or to more than one? Feel free to stop and pursue any that your curiosity is stimulating.

- Sacrifice
- Worship
- Conformed
- Transformed
- Prove
- Perfect

Did you notice there is an echo of the Hebrew Scriptures with the word "sacrifice"? Did you hear it? Does the echo lead you to a mental image of giving an animal in sacrifice to God at the altar in front of the temple? In contrast, Paul urges each of us to be a "living and holy sacrifice." In ancient Israel the sacrifice was an unblemished firstborn animal. When we offer ourselves to God in service, we must also be unblemished and holy. Of course, the sacrifice in ancient Israel was a dead animal. With ironic humor, Paul exclaims that we are to be a living sacrifice. What does it mean to be a living sacrifice? I will leave this question for you to ponder.

You may also have been drawn to the word "conformed," which is the way the world influences God's people by shaping them in ungodly ways. I have an image of a potter working with wet clay. The final product is a clay pot that represents us. When we are conformed to the world, this clay pot has been shaped by the god of this world, who is the potter.

I was not led to "conformed," but my curiosity drew me to "transformed." We are transformed, or changed, by the renewing of our minds. I will now ask you to conduct a word study on "transformed."

- Using biblehub.com, what is the original Greek word?
- How many times does the Greek word appear in the New Testament?
- List each of the four verses, and take brief notes on how the word is used in each verse.

Now try your best to see a pattern (theme or main idea) that emerges from these four verses.

What does it Mean to be "Transformed"?

I trust you used biblehub.com to look up the Greek word, which is μεταμορφόω (*metamorphoo*). Can you guess the English word that comes from *metamorphoo*? It is "metamorphosis," the process that a caterpillar undergoes in various stages as it changes to become a beautiful butterfly. Strong's English definition simply says "to change the form or transform," which is totally inadequate for our purpose to penetrate a depth of meaning in Scripture. So, I trust you went to the right column of the concordance page, noted that the Greek word appears only four times, and then you scrolled down to make a list of the four verses. You then read each verse in its context and took brief notes on how the word was being used.

If you are a deductive thinker, you probably already saw a pattern simply by reading the four verses in their context, although you must now struggle to fully appreciate the details to support your thoughts. If you are an inductive thinker, you will undoubtedly enjoy digging into the details of the four verses, but I suspect you will struggle to uncover the pattern. I will proceed in an inductive manner by taking one verse at a time to perceive a depth of meaning in each verse before considering a pattern.

I will apply a principle that was proposed by the Jewish sages, which I have found to be quite relevant in this process of

Word Study, Patterns, and Sharing Discoveries | 113

word study. That is, not only does God mark the first appearance of a word as relevant, but He also places these words in an order that will offer a significant meaning. I will now follow this principle of first appearance and order of appearance in order to examine the four verses in the order in which they appear.

> Matthew 17:2
> Mark 9:2
> Romans 12:2
> 2 Corinthians 3:18

The first appearance is about the transfiguration of Yeshua, which is found in two of the gospels, Matthew and Mark. We will look at these two verses as one account. However, before we begin you must remove from your mind any English words of translation. Remember, all translations are interpretation. So, let the original words of Scripture reveal their meaning to you.

I will now focus on the physical change that occurred. Yeshua's face "shone like the sun, and his garments became as white as light" (Mat 17:2). Mark tells us, "his garments became radiant and exceedingly white, as no launderer on earth can whiten them." I suggest that this transfiguration is prophetic of some future time when the children of God will be able to come into God's presence without sin.

God's righteousness is conveyed metaphorically as all light. There is no darkness in Him. Sin is represented by darkness. If we try to come into the presence of God in a sinful condition, we will be obliterated, killed and destroyed by the brilliance of His light. Yeshua, His son, *can* enter into His presence because Yeshua is without sin. We also will be without sin. Yeshua is leading us there now, and will present us in righteousness at some time in the future.

Perhaps it will be helpful for you to consider similar imagery in Isaiah, who portrays this future time.

> Your sun will no longer set, nor will your moon wane; for you will have the Lord for an everlasting light, and the days of your mourning will be over.
> Is 60:20

Returning now to our word study on μεταμορφόω, we see that Yeshua's transfiguration and Isaiah's words of prophecy teach us about something that is still future. "The days of your mourning" are caused by separation from God, which sin produces. However, at some time in the future (we do not know when) God's children will be able to stand in His glorious presence because they will be without sin in righteousness. Therefore, the transfiguration of Yeshua prophecies of something still future. Yeshua was changed, or transfigured, so "His face shone like the sun, and His garments became as white as light" (Mat 17:2). Yet, we are going to learn from our word study that it is possible to bring this future relationship with God into our lives today.

In both accounts of the transfiguration, Matthew and Mark, God spoke out of a cloud with these words. "This is My beloved son in whom I am well pleased. Listen to him!" Unfortunately I think we fail to fully appreciate the intimate relationship between Father and son that this transfiguration conveys, a relationship that is available to us also. Furthermore, I think we need to consider the three disciples who were standing in the light of God, which is prophetic of a future time. Yet, this account portrays more than what is still future. It suggests that we can stand in righteousness today. Our word study will help us understand this powerful principle.

We turn now to the next appearance of our word, which occurs in the verse where we began.

> Do not be conformed to this world, but be transformed by the renewing of your mind, so that you may prove what the will of God is, that which is good and acceptable and perfect. Rom 12:2

We must keep in mind the first appearance if we are going to see the pattern. In the gospel account of the transfiguration, Yeshua shone with the light of God in a prophetic way that pointed to the future when he would come into the presence of the Father and be seated with our Lord Yeshua. Yeshua could only be seated at the right hand of the Father in a righteous condition, that is, without sin. Yet, we are intrigued by the three disciples who were also standing in the light of God without being destroyed.

In his letter to the Romans, Paul is helping us understand that we can come into the presence of God in a righteous condition now, and he tells us how. We renew our minds. That is, we bring the life and light of God into our inner thoughts when we put the Word of God in our minds and hearts. This is not a simple step or a click of the fingers. It is a process of growing in the light of God through the study of His Word, and putting that understanding into our daily lives. However, the important point for our pattern is this. It is possible, according to Paul, for us to come into the presence of God in a holy condition in our lives today *if* we grow in our knowledge of Him.

Are you ready for the last of our four verses, which I guarantee will leave you breathless? We will work through it together, using our ancient methods of penetrating a depth of meaning.

> ¹⁷Now the Lord is the Spirit, and where the Spirit of the Lord is, *there* is liberty.
> 18 But we all, with unveiled face, beholding as in a mirror the glory of the Lord, are being transformed into the same image from glory to glory, just as from the Lord, the Spirit. 2 Co 3:17-18

Let us begin with an echo. Did you hear it? Again it is Paul who is conveying this echo, this time to the Corinthians. He is encouraging all of us to come before the Lord with an unveiled face. Now, the temple had two veils. The first covered the entrance to the Temple where a priest came into what was called the Holy Place. This is where the menorah and showbread and altar of incense were located. Only priests could enter this part of the temple to replenish the lamps each day with oil, place new showbread on the table of His presence each week, and add incense and wood to the altar of incense. Priests had to be holy to perform this service.

After passing through the Holy Place, a second veil separated the Holy Place from the Holy of Holies, which was the innermost part of the temple where the presence of God hovered over the Ark of the Covenant. Only the high priest could pass through this second veil to enter the Holy of Holies, and then only once a year on Yom Kippur, the Day of Atonement. Thus, only once a year the high priest was in the presence of the most Holy God.

So, what does Paul tell us? He first reminds us that "the Lord is the Spirit." How, then, can we come into the presence of this Spirit in an unholy condition? But wait a minute! We have just learned that we can become good and acceptable and perfect by renewing our minds with the Word of God, at least in part and from time to time. Therefore, Paul is now leading us one step farther. When we change from the way the world has shaped us to a holy and righteous condition by renewing our minds, we can metaphorically pass through the second veil into the presence of God. We are being transformed into God's image, which is Spirit. We can enter the light of His presence in righteousness because we have been transformed into His image.

Now comes the most astonishing and exciting part of what Paul is telling us. He instructs us to look in a mirror. What do we see? Do we see ourselves as the world has shaped us, or do we see God. The purpose of the veil in the temple was to separate mankind from God because they could not come into His presence in a sinful condition. However, if our face is unveiled, we have direct access to God. Yet, we must be righteous without sin because we are coming into the presence of the righteous God.

Now we come to the pinnacle of this verse in 2 Corinthians 3:18, which takes us beyond renewing our minds. In our process of change, Paul tells us we are being transformed "from glory to glory." These beautiful words can only be understood in the context of the Hebraic sense of time. In the beginning God created us in His image, which is righteous (Gen 1:27). That is the first glory. The final glory is still future when we will come before God in a completely righteous condition. However, now we can be transformed by restoring God's original creation into our lives today. We can make the future kingdom a reality when we walk in righteousness. That is Paul's second glory. We are transformed from the glory of God in the beginning to the glory of God we are becoming.

What has happened to enable this tremendous leap forward? We see that we have been transformed, transfigured and changed into the image of God. What is that image? It is Spirit without form. It is righteous and holy without sin. We have gone from the glory of God when we first became His children through our faith in His son, to the glory of God that can transform, transfigure and change us into God's image. This is a life that is filled with His Spirit.

Revealing the Pattern

Consider now the pattern that you first saw as you thought about your notes on μεταμορφόω. You could see how this Greek word was being used in all four verses where it appears in the New Testament. What pattern did you see?

From this word study, I see an ascending pattern from the order in which the word appears in Scripture. First, in Matthew and Mark we must come to know Yeshua as our Savior, and then as our Lord and Master. Who is he? What does he represent? What has his transfiguration revealed to us?

Next, from Paul's words to the Romans, we see that we can grow in our understanding of God, the Father, through our study of His Word. This will be a lifelong journey as our Lord Yeshua leads us and the Holy Spirit guides us. Although we cannot arrive into the presence of God in a complete way in our lives today, Paul exhorts us to be transformed as a holy sacrifice to God that is good and acceptable and perfect. So, something must be possible now. I sometimes explain that "God only sees the heart," so it is our heart we must cultivate. Furthermore, we realize that we can come into God's presence in a righteous condition now, but only "from time to time and not all the time."

Finally, in the last verse in Corinthians we came to the pinnacle of this ascending pattern. As we grow in righteousness we must learn to see ourselves as God sees us. He is a loving Father who is all positive, all light, and all that is true. In Him there is no negative, no darkness, and no falsehood or deceit. He created us in His image! The world, on the other hand, does everything in its power to have us dwell on our faults, and to form our thoughts as negative and critical, not positive and uplifting. The world may be shaping us in its image, which is darkness generated by deceit, but we can change that image and become the new creation through our Lord Yeshua and the guiding presence of the Holy Spirit.

Let me conclude my thoughts by sharing with you a wonderful picture. An adorable calico kitten is sitting in front of a mirror. What does the kitten see? He sees reflected in the mirror, not a meek kitten, but a powerful and roaring lion. That is you. You can see yourself as God sees you, which is a child of a loving Father. Together with His son, Yeshua the Messiah, you are growing into His image. And guess what? You become what you see and believe.

Sharing Your Discovery

If you are a deductive thinker, you are probably eager to share your global thoughts with others. After all, these general ideas have generated your own excitement, and God certainly wants you to witness what you have discovered. However, you must support your ideas with evidence from Scripture, which is the purpose of the list of verses that contain the word that first caught your attention. If you fail to give detailed support, you will just be promoting a personal theology that others will likely dismiss.

If you are an inductive thinker, you were undoubtedly excited about the details you uncovered from your word study. You will be tempted to share these details. However, others will be confused unless you first start with a main idea, which is the pattern you have uncovered. Then you can support your main idea with the details. If you fail to first offer a general concept to which the details can attach, your presentation will become a confusing mass of facts.

So, how do you share your discoveries? In all cases, regardless of whether you are a deductive or inductive thinker, you must present a general idea first, which is sometimes called a thesis or a proposal. This general idea is the pattern you have seen from your study of the details. But don't stop there. Then you must support your proposal with evidence from Scripture. You already have this evidence. It is in the list of verses and the brief notes you took during your word study.

Chapter Nine
Unraveling a Chiastic Construction

In this session, I will show you how to unravel a puzzling passage that cannot be read as simple prose because it is a chiastic construction. I will offer as an example Romans 10:9-10, which Paul has constructed in an exquisite artistic pattern that conveys an incredible depth of meaning. You will learn to recognize the chiastic pattern that Paul presents in these verses by listening for repetition that forms parallel lines.

What is Chiasm?

Chiasm is an ancient literary device that is common throughout Scripture. Scholars have long recognized chiasm in the literature of ancient Greece, but only recently has their attention been drawn to the prevalence and richness of chiasm in both the Old and the New Testaments.

Chiasm is constructed with parallel lines that point to a chiastic center. In Session Three, you worked on parallel lines in Hebrew poetry. There you discovered that parallel lines are often connected by using the same word or concept, which is a form of repetition. The result can be a powerful artistic meaning that emerges from the relationship between the parallel lines that all point to a chiastic center.

For example, let us briefly review by considering the first two verses of Psalm 6.

> A^1 O Lord, do not rebuke me in Your anger,
> A^2 Nor chasten me in Your wrath.
>
> B^1 Be gracious to me, O Lord, for I am pining away;
> B^2 Heal me, O Lord, for my bones are dismayed.
>
> Ps 6:1-2

Rebuke and chasten in the A lines mean essentially the same thing. Anger and wrath in the A lines are also connected by a similar meaning. Thus, the two A lines in are a parallel construction formed by repetition. In this case, the repetition heightens the intensity of David's guilt. Now you will practice identifying the parallel nature of the next two B lines.

- What is the relationship between "be gracious" and "heal me"? (Hint: It is not similarity).
- What is the relationship between "pining away" and "bones are dismayed"?
- The most important relationship is between "God's grace" and "pining away," which is reinforced by "God's healing power" and "bones that are dismayed." Before explaining this relationship, stop to look up the Hebrew word translated "pining away," and uncover its meaning with a word study.
- Now explain the powerful meaning conveyed by this parallel construction of the B lines.

I trust you took the time to do this work. I will not share my thoughts (the Hebraic way of teaching prompts you to arrive at your own conclusions), but will move on to explain a chiastic construction.

A Simple Example of Chiasm

The most simple chiastic structure is commonly labeled ABA. That is, the two A lines are parallel, and line B is the chiastic center. Consider the ABA construction from the Parable of the Prodigal Son. Start by reading the A lines first.

A^1 "I am no longer worthy to be called your son; make me as one of your hired men."
    B. So he got up and came to his father. But while he was still a long way off, his father saw him and felt compassion for him, and ran and embraced him and kissed him.
A^2 And the son said to him, "Father, I have sinned against heaven and in your sight; I am no longer worthy to be called your son." Lk 15:19-21

Did you hear the repetition? In the first A line the prodigal son declares, "I am no longer worthy to be called your son." In the second A line the prodigal son again declares, "I am no longer worthy to be called your son." These can be viewed as two parallel A lines that are pointing to the chiastic center, which is the B line.

There are now three things you must consider in this chiastic construction. I will not ask you to attempt answers at this time. Simply ponder the questions.

- What is the relationship between the two parallel A lines?
- What is the echo from the Hebrew Scriptures when the prodigal son declares, "I am no longer worthy"?
- What is the significance of the central B line to which the parallel lines are pointing?

The startling relationship of the A lines is caused by a deletion (something has been omitted) and by an expansion (something has been added). In another sense, we might say that one thing has been replaced by another. Do you see it?

- What makes the two A lines parallel? That is, what is the expression that has been repeated?
- What is different about the two A lines? That is, what has been deleted and what has been added?
- The relationship between the two A lines is in this difference. What is the relationship?

The two A lines repeat the phrase, "I am no longer worthy." In a minute you will see that this repetition is an echo that will lead you to the Hebrew Scriptures. But first let us look at what is different in these two lines.

In the first A line we hear, "I am not worthy; make me as one of your hired men." In the second A line the request to become a hired servant has been replaced by "I have sinned against heaven and in your sight," which is repentance. When the prodigal son repented, he was no longer degraded in the lowly position of a hired servant but was worthy of the status of a son. Stop now and re-read Luke 15:19-21.

Now we will turn to the echo, which is from the Jacob story. Jacob had left Laban, his father-in-law, and had taken with him his two wives, his two concubines, 11 sons (Benjamin had not yet been born), one daughter (Dinah), and all his animals and hired servants. As he was about to reenter the Promised Land after 20 difficult years of exile in a foreign country, Jacob had to face his brother, Esau, from whom he had purchased the birthright and had subsequently stolen the blessing that accompanied the birthright. Jacob humbled himself before God and spoke these words. "I am unworthy of all the lovingkindness and of all the faithfulness which You have shown to Your servant" (Gen 32:10). The Parable of the Prodigal Son is a commentary on this story of Jacob.

Before we continue, you can now reflect on the Jacob story and all of its parallels to the Parable of the Prodigal Son. You will see that there is much more than Jacob's words about being unworthy.

- What was the relationship of the two brothers, Jacob and Esau, in the Jacob story? What was the relationship of the two brothers in the Parable of the Prodigal Son?
- What was the cause and nature of Jacob's exile? What was the cause and nature of the exile of the Prodigal Son?
- What led Jacob to return to the land of Israel? What led the prodigal son to return to his father?

We can turn now to the chiastic center. I have taken the one verse that we labeled B, and divided it into two parts. B¹ is about the prodigal son. B² is about the father.

> B¹ So he [the prodigal son] got up [ἀνίστημι *anistemi*] and came to his father.
> B² But while he was still a long way off, his father saw him and felt compassion *for him*, and ran and embraced him and kissed him. Luke 15:20

Let us look at the prodigal son first. The English translation reads "he got up," which totally misses the impact of the passage. A common Greek word for standing for God is ἵστημι. However, our verse has added a preposition as a prefix meaning "up" (ἀνά). Thus, the prodigal son is not only standing for God (his father represents God), but he is standing *up* for God (ἀνίστημι).

Now we turn to the father. The rhythm of multiple actions is powerful. He *saw* and *felt* and *ran* and *embraced* and *kissed*. For even greater emphasis, the father did these things when the son "was still a long way off." Can you visualize the picture and feel the emotion?

The father of the prodigal son represents God whose loving forgiveness remains open and available (as we saw earlier with Cain). God is urging us to repent and, as He instructed Cain, "to do well." When we turn to the Lord with a love that displays a humble heart desiring to submit and obey, we are returned to the loving arms of our Father.

Tackling a Puzzling Passage

Now that you have reviewed parallel lines and learned about the ancient literary device of chiasm, you are ready to tackle a provocative passage. It is provocative and puzzling because these two verses have led to two possible interpretations that are polar opposites.

> [9] If you confess with your mouth Jesus *as* Lord, and believe in your heart that God raised Him from the dead, you will be saved;
> [10] for with the heart a person believes, resulting in righteousness, and with the mouth he confesses, resulting in salvation. Rom 10:9-10

You undoubtedly recognize this passage, which has become the central proselytizing message of the evangelical Christian movement. Simply believe in your heart that God raised Jesus from the dead and you will be saved.[9] However, there are numerous strange and puzzling aspects in these two verses. There is an "if" clause that has led to another interpretation. "If you

---

[9] For the "once saved, always saved" position, see Matthew Correll, *Faith in Christ is Eternal Life: Understanding God's Free Grace* (Fulfillment Press, 2009).

confess with your mouth the Lord Jesus" conveys a requirement to make Jesus lord in your life.[10] So, what is required to be saved?

No matter which position you take (or any variety of these two opposing interpretations) I always suggest that you first anchor yourself in your traditional understanding of what this passage means. Carefully review what you believe. Consider what has led you to this conclusion and the evidence for your belief. After all, you do not want to be blown about by winds of doctrine, and I do not want you jumping on what I am going to propose. Instead, you should seriously consider the evidence before drawing a conclusion. The evidence I will be presenting views these verses as a chiastic construction with tantalizing relationships between the parallel lines, and between the parallel lines and the chiastic center.

You should begin by carefully stating your traditional understanding of the meaning of these verses. You may wish to share these perspectives with a study partner or in a small group discussion.

Now consider the questions below so you can understand why I propose that this passage is puzzling. I suggest you do not try to answer these questions just yet because you are still focused on your traditional understanding. So, simply consider the puzzling aspect of the two verses.

- Are there two requirements to be saved, confessing Jesus as Lord and believing in your heart that God raised him from the dead?
- Or, is there just one requirement, which is to believe in the resurrection, or perhaps simply believe in Jesus the Messiah?
- Is there a difference between "resulting in righteousness" and "resulting in salvation?"
- What does the mouth represent, and what does the heart represent?

---

[10] John MacArthur is a prolific writer and speaker who has promoted what has come to be called "Lordship Salvation." That is, one must make Jesus Lord in his or her life in order to be saved. John MacArthur, *Right Thinking in a World Gone Wrong* (Harvest House, 2009).

- Why is "you will be saved" in verse 9 repeated in verse 10 as "resulting in salvation?"

These are legitimate and troubling questions, but I pose them now simply to show you how puzzling this passage really is. Following the inductive approach, we will unravel the linguistic details before attempting to see the interpretive pattern.

Did you hear the repetition? Read these verses again and listen to the repetition.

> [9] If you confess with your mouth Jesus *as* Lord, and believe in your heart that God raised Him from the dead, you will be saved;
> [10] for with the heart a person believes, resulting in righteousness, and with the mouth he confesses, resulting in salvation. Rom 10:9-10

Repetition may indicate the presence of chiasm, but not always. So, now we must consider the possibility of a chiastic composition by composing it in its artistic construction of parallel lines. The chiastic construction of this passage, which is generated by repetition, is actually ABCBA. So, let me show you what I perceive as the chiastic pattern.

> A^1 If you confess with your mouth Jesus *as* Lord,
> $\quad B^1$ and believe in your heart that God raised Him from the dead,
> $\quad\quad$ C. you will be saved;
> $\quad B^2$ for with the heart a person believes, resulting in righteousness,
> A^2 and with the mouth he confesses, resulting in salvation.

Now it is time to analyze the chiasm in the same manner that we did previously with the Parable of the Prodigal Son. Try answering the questions first before considering my thoughts.

Analyzing the Chiasm

- What is the relationship between the two parallel A lines?

Do you see the repetition of "mouth" and "confess," which makes the lines parallel? However, what is most important is the *relationship* between the two A lines. The second A line has expanded with additional information, which is the result of confessing Jesus as Lord. That is, when we submit in obedience to him as our Lord and Master, the result is "salvation."

- What is the relationship between the two parallel B lines?

Again we have a repetition, this time of "believing in your heart." However, what is the *relationship* between the two B lines? The second line again gives the result, which is "righteousness." Righteousness is the condition without sin that is required for us to come into God's presence.

Now we come to the chiastic center, which is the heart of the passage. However, this C line is puzzling. We read, "You will be saved." But isn't "salvation" also present in the second A line? So, what is the relationship between "you will be saved" (C) and "resulting in salvation" (A^2)? We cannot answer this last question without understanding the Hebraic sense of time. So we will stop now to consider the Hebraic sense of time.

The Answer is in the Hebraic Sense of Time

We have been brought up with the Greek sense of time, which is linear. That is, the past is behind us, and we can only access the past through written records, archaeological artifacts, or oral history. The past does not exist in the present except by memory. Furthermore, in linear time, the future is ahead of us. We can only access the future through imagination, so the future does not exist except through our creative thought. Therefore, the only things we can experience in reality are in the present. In the Greek sense of time we tend to live primarily in the present, not in the past nor in the future.

Not so with the Hebraic sense of time because God created time and is in time. Thus, God is present in all aspects of time. To the extent that we are with God, we can also be in all aspects of time – past, present and future.

Let me give you an example. Are you familiar with the Passover Haggadah that is read each year on Passover Eve? This creative narrative retells the story of the Exodus from Egypt in a way that makes God's past deliverance seem very real as well as meaningful to one's current life. The past event becomes as real to the listeners as if it were happening at that very moment. The past becomes real in the life of the listeners.

Let me give you another example of the Hebraic sense of time that perceives God in all aspects of time. The creation account occurred "in the beginning," that is, in past linear time. From our Greek perspective we can only experience it by reading the first chapters of Genesis. However, let me explain something about the way this creation account is conveyed in the Hebrew text.

Biblical Hebrew does not have numerous nuances of time like we have in English (is doing, was doing, will do, might do, has done, might have done, etc.). Hebrew conveys time either as complete or incomplete. Now listen to Scripture describing the creation account. Listen to its completed sense of time.

> A. By the seventh day God completed His work which He had done,
>> B. and He rested on the seventh day from all His work which He had done.
>>> C. Then God blessed the seventh day and sanctified it, because
>> B. in it He rested from all His work
> A. which God had created and made. Gen 2:2-3

First, let me offer a few observations.

- God "completed" His work of creation in the beginning.
- "Rest" conveys the completion of work.
- "Made" is the same Hebrew word that is translated "done," so we might read, "He rested from all His work that God had 'created' and 'done.'"

From the Hebraic perspective of the creation, which is conveyed through the Hebrew language, is there any question in your mind that God's creation is completely complete? In addition to the completed sense of time, the concept of "rest" in Hebrew conveys the end of all work, thus nothing is left to be done. Yet, look at me, and look at yourself. Are you complete without sin, thus completely righteous? Am I? I don't think so. Yet, we are part of God's creation that was finished on the seventh day of creation and is now complete.

For those who were raised in the Greek sense of time, this understanding of God's completed work in the beginning may seem confusing. I like to explain it this way. If God says that something is finished, even though we see its completion in the future, we can consider it done because "God is not a man who lies" (Num 29:13). We should live in God's finished work as a present reality *if* we understand the Hebrew sense of time. This is how the Passover Haggadah is read. A past event becomes living and real each year on Passover Eve. We bring the past into a present reality.

Now let us turn to the future. If you are Greek-oriented with a western sense of time, the future is probably fuzzy and perhaps not worth thinking about. However, God has given us glimpses of the future when we will come into His presence in righteousness. We can (and should) live in the absolute certainty of this future restoration of the Garden of Eden. This idyllic image and the life it conveys was a completed reality a long time ago in the Garden of Eden. However, we can bring the past into our lives now, so the future fulfillment becomes a reality when we walk with God in righteousness in our lives today. It is possible to be one with God without sin, that is, from time to time. Sin caused the original separation between God and His created beings, but God is in the process of restoring the unity between God and His created beings.

At this point, let me introduce a caveat. We cannot live at complete rest with God all the time. We cannot be one with God all the time. We cannot be without sin all the time. Yet, for those who belong to God through their faith in Christ, they have been given the gift of the Holy Spirit. So, when they walk in the love and faith of Christ, they activate this gift which enables them to be one with God. Walking with God only happens from time to time because we still live in a sinful world. However, it is possible to be one with God at times, and we should live with that expectation.

There is one more aspect about the Hebraic sense of time that we must address before returning to our chiastic structure in Romans 10:9-10. In our western tradition of time, we tend to blow out of proportion the fall of Adam and Eve and the sinful nature of mankind. We cannot grasp Genesis 1:27: "God created mankind in in His image." We tend to conclude that the righteousness of God's creation has been destroyed only to be restored at some time in the future. Not so with the Hebraic sense of time.

Since God is with us in all senses of time, He sees us as righteous in all aspects of time – past, present and future. Listen again to what He tells us. "God created man in His own image, in the image of God He created him; male and female He created them" (Gen 1:27). "Created" is in the completed sense of Hebraic time. God has completed righteousness in us. Thus, from the beginning mankind has been righteous in God's eyes.

Now turn to the future, which we know from the Hebraic sense of time can be present with us now if we simply believe it and claim it. We know that in the end of time we will become completely righteous in order to enter God's presence. However, when we walk in that understanding now, we become what God has created in us.

Returning to the Chiasm in Romans 10:9-10

Paul applies the Hebraic sense of time to the concept of salvation as follows:

- You were saved (free from sin and one with God) from the beginning of creation.
- When you first believed in God's son, you were righteous in His eyes with the promise of salvation.
- Even though we will experience periods of pain and suffering throughout our lives, when we walk in righteousness we are rescued from the pain and suffering caused by the world. We become one with God and at rest with Him.

- God is present in all aspects of time. Since God is with you, you are also present with God in all aspects of time.

Now let us return to the chiastic structure as Paul wants us to understand the concept of salvation.

A^1 If you confess with your mouth Jesus *as* Lord,
    B^1 and believe in your heart that God raised
    Him from the dead,
        C. you will be saved;
    B^2 for with the heart a person believes,
    resulting in righteousness,
A^2 and with the mouth he confesses,
  resulting in salvation.

Let us start with the chiastic center. The central point that Paul is making is about the concept of salvation. However, there are two parallel B lines that have a relationship to this chiastic center, and two parallel A lines that also have a relationship to the concept of salvation. The B lines are closest to the chiastic center, and therefore they command the most privileged position. We will begin with the B lines.

If we believe that God raised His son from the dead, there is an important result called "righteousness." That is, when you first believe in Yeshua, God sees you as righteous and you belong to Him. You are His child and He is your Father. In fact, God declared you righteous from the beginning, and you will stand before Him in righteousness in the end of times. But what about now? That is the important question for us to be asking, and we must turn to the A lines for the answer.

We remember that the B lines have the most privileged position because they are closest to the chiastic center. The A lines are farther away, and there is an interesting reason why. All God's children are righteous in His eyes with the promise of future eternal life with Him (the A lines). Those who belong to God by their faith in His son are large in number. As we move to the B lines, only some of God's children confess Jesus as Lord, submitting to him in humble obedience and serving God in His kingdom. For those who confess Jesus as Lord, the result is "salvation" (the B lines).

We need to stop once more and focus on the Greek word that has been translated "saved" and "salvation." There is only one Greek word (σῴζω *sozo*). However (and this is a big "however"), there are two aspects of meaning for the one Greek word *sozo*.

First we are saved (rescued) from death, the penalty for sin, by God's promise of future salvation, which is expressed in the A lines. All of God's children have that promise. All of God's children are saved from the penalty of death, which is a promise of something future. However, we can live in that promise in our lives today if we choose.

Second, we are saved, or rescued, from the consequences of walking in the ways of the world when we walk in the ways of God. What does the world give us? Pain and suffering in our daily lives. God, on the other hand, gives us a daily salvation that is better translated as "wholeness." We can be made whole in Him by a walk of righteousness. We can be at rest in Him. We can share in His glory. We can be one with Him, no longer separated by sin.

This second aspect of salvation, which is wholeness in our daily lives, is conveyed by the B lines. We can only claim this walk of wholeness when we make Yeshua Lord in our lives, and submit in obedience to a godly way of living. Because those who make Yeshua Lord are a smaller number of God's children, they are described in the A lines that are farthest from the chiastic center.

The chiastic center, then, which is expressed in the C line, captures both concepts of salvation. Closest to the chiastic center, and applying to all God's children, is the promise of coming into His presence, which requires a righteous condition (the A lines). This is a promise of something future. Farther away from the chiastic center, which applies only to some of God's children, is the rescue (or salvation) from pain and suffering that is caused by walking in the ways of the world (the B lines). Those who make Yeshua Lord are made whole, and become one with God in their daily walk with Him.

As you conduct your daily Bible study, you will begin to see chiastic constructions all over Scripture. You will be alerted to these passages by repetition. Take time to stop and put the verses in their artistic pattern. Then you can begin posing questions about relationships. I think you will be surprised and pleased.

Chapter Ten
What to do with a Citation

In Session Seven you practiced listening in New Testament passages to echoes (allusions) from the Hebrew Scriptures. In fact, the New Testament is teeming with these echoes which we can explain in three ways.

First, we must remember that the New Testament had not yet been written at the time of Yeshua. Yet, dramatic things were happening that seemed to be a fulfillment of Old Testament prophecies. The promised Messiah had arrived, and he was performing miracles. Then he was crucified and resurrected out from the dead. What did all this mean? The first Christians turned to the Hebrew Scriptures to understand what was happening. With great excitement they told others about this fulfillment of Old Testament prophecy.

Second, the authors of the New Testament were, in large part, Jews who knew the Hebrew Scriptures intimately. They had memorized these sacred writings from the time they were small children, and the Holy Writings had become the pattern for their daily lives as well as their source of information about God.

Third, people in first century Israel believed that God had given them everything in His Word that they would ever need to know. There was a plain and simple meaning (*p'shat*), but there was also a mysterious depth of meaning (*midrash*) that could be uncovered by those whose hearts yearned to grow close to God.

In this session, you will be working with direct citations of the Hebrew Scriptures that are found in the New Testament. You have heard me say that there are over 300 of these quotations. Your first challenge will be to recognize these citations, and then you must know what to do with them. You will be learning how to respond as the people at the time of Yeshua would have responded.

How to Recognize a Citation

People at the time of Yeshua would have "heard" the citations. However, we have not internalized Scripture by memorization as they had. Therefore, we need a good reference Bible that records the citations in small capital letters and then identifies the Old Testament verse in the middle or bottom margin.

I use (and recommend) the New American Standard Bible Reference Edition both because its goal is to translate as closely to the original text as possible and because it does a good job of identifying citations. However, there are other Reference Bibles which do something similar that you may choose to use. It is very important that you have a good reference Bible so you can recognize citations when they occur, and you know where to go in the Hebrew Scriptures to find that citation.

Recovering the Memorized Block

Based on my work with New Testament quotations from the Old Testament, I have concluded that a brief citation would have stimulated the memorized block in the minds of early listeners. After all, in oral societies that preserve the history of their people, memorization does not occur in small pieces like single verses, but in thematic blocks. This suggestion became a breakthrough for my understanding of citations in the New Testament.

Therefore, when we see a citation we must first find that verse in the Hebrew Scriptures, and then we must identify its context which will probably be the memorized block. We have worked on context in Session Seven, which is the surrounding verses that project one main idea. We will never know the exact memorized blocks of the ancient Israelites, but context offers a block that contains one thematic idea.

After identifying and reading the cited verse in its context in the Hebrew Scriptures, which we assume is the likely memorized block, you must then compare the citation in the New Testament with what it has cited in the Hebrew Scriptures. Remember that people of ancient Israel "listened" to the text, and they would have "heard" any change or difference.

I first learned that these changes were most likely intentional from my intensive work on the writings of Paul. Paul often deletes part of a verse, or adds something, or makes a subtle change in his citation. The early Christians would have "heard" these differences, and in the difference will be some kind of clue to a deeper meaning.

It is now time for us to practice listening and responding to a citation as the people of ancient Israel would have done.

Citation in the Parable of the Mustard Seed

We all know the parable of the mustard seed. A tiny seed grows into a large tree, and we learn that we can also be spiritually large and strong if we are with God. However, did you ever stop to ponder and work the citation that is displayed in capital letters? Do you know how to find this verse in the Hebrew Scriptures? As you read this passage below, take special note of how the citation is integrated into the parable.

> ³¹'The kingdom of heaven is like a mustard seed, which a man took and sowed in his field;
> ³² and this is smaller than all *other* seeds, but when it is full grown, it is larger than the garden plants and becomes a tree, so that THE BIRDS OF THE AIR come and NEST IN ITS BRANCHES." Mat 13:31-32; cf. Mk 4:31-32; Lk 13:19

The parable is recorded in Matthew, but also appears in Mark 4:31-32 and Luke 13:19. I always select one gospel account rather than trying to understand any changes or evidence of editing among the different gospels. In this case, I have selected the passage in Matthew because it is the longest and because it has the most artistic rendering.

The capital letters indicate a citation. THE BIRDS OF THE AIR come and NEST IN ITS BRANCHES. The middle margin of the NASB identifies the citation as Ezekiel 17:23.

Let me stop for a moment and comment on the purpose of all the New Testament parables. If you have read my book, *Uncovering Mysteries of the Kingdom: Viewing the Parables as Haggadic Midrish*, you have considered my suggestion that all the parables are a form of haggadic midrash, which discloses deeper understanding from the Hebrew Scriptures by re-telling a biblical narrative in an artistic way. Thus, haggadic midrash is a form of commentary on the Hebrew Scriptures.

You will remember that we worked on the Parable of the Prodigal Son in the last chapter. We discovered that this parable is a commentary on the story of Jacob, who returned to the land of Israel after 20 years of exile in a foreign land. Words spoken by the prodigal son to his father ("I am no longer worthy to be called your son" Lk 15:21), are an echo of words that Jacob declared to God. "I am unworthy of all the lovingkindness and of all the faithfulness which You have shown to Your servant" (Gen 32:10). Thus, the Parable of the Prodigal Son is a form of haggadic midrash on the account of Jacob.

As we return now to the Parable of the Mustard Seed, you should start by re-reading these two verses in Matthew 13:32-33. What catches your attention and causes you to stop and ponder? Try answering this question now, and we will discuss it together later.

Now you are ready to turn to the cited verse, Ezekiel 17:23, which is the connection to the Hebrew Scriptures. As haggadic midrash, the citation in this parable and the words that surround it will create some kind of commentary on the Ezekiel passage. Read the cited verse in Ezekiel, but keep your finger in Matthew because you are going to be flipping back and forth between Matthew and Ezekiel. We will begin in Matthew as we work to uncover the purpose of this citation and the meaning that results.

- The citation in Matthew is not exactly the same as the verse in Ezekiel. Why do you think the translators selected Ezekiel 17:23 as the likely verse in the Hebrew Scriptures that the parable is citing?
- If Scripture was memorized in blocks, then we must identify the likely block in Ezekiel in which the cited verse is located. We will never know for certain, but at the very least we must ask, "What is the context of Ezekiel 17:23?" That is, what verses do you think constitute the context? As we proceed I will call this context "the block." What verses do you think constitute the block?

We often make a distinction between the immediate context and the larger context. The larger context would probably be the memorized block. The immediate context is a smaller portion that contains a smaller sub-idea within the larger context. Do you agree with me that the immediate context is Ezekiel 17:22-

24? The greater context probably begins in Ezekiel 17:11. Stop now and re-read both the greater and the immediate context.

God's Language of Judgment

The language of judgment in this passage in Ezekiel is quite strong. God's wrath seems to be directed primarily against the king of Judah (most likely Jehoiachin). However, remember that God is also referring to the people as "the rebellious house." Therefore, the judgment against Judah's leader will also fall on the rebellious people. As the Babylonians were approaching and threatening to conquer Jerusalem, God employed this intense language of judgment to urge the people to repent and depend solely on Him. Listen now to this language of judgment.

> "I will spread My net over him [Jehoiachin], and he will be caught in My snare. Then I will bring him to Babylon and enter into judgment with him there *regarding* the unfaithful act which he has committed against Me [Jehoiachin was relying on Egypt for help instead of relying on God]."
>
> [21] "All the choice men in all his troops will fall by the sword, and the survivors will be scattered to every wind; and you will know that I, the Lord, have spoken." Ez 17:20-21

This judgment did indeed happen. King Jehoiachin was taken into captivity to Babylon where he died. King Zedekiah was then placed on the throne in Jerusalem but he too turned to the Egyptians for help. So, the Babylonians returned to destroy the city of Jerusalem and its temple, and to take the people into captivity to Babylon.

Because of the prevalence of this language of judgment in the Hebrew Scriptures, Christians often think that the God of the Old Testament is a God of wrath and judgment, whereas the God of the New Testament is a God of love and compassion. There almost seems to be two Gods, one for Israel and one for believers in Christ, or at least one God who treats his children quite differently. This conclusion results, in part, from a literal reading that fails to perceive the intentional linguistic artistry of the text. We need to think Hebrew, not Greek.

Linguistic Artistry in Ezekiel

Let us begin now to penetrate the artistry of the language in Ezekiel 17:22-24 before returning to Matthew. Read these three verses carefully, almost to the point of memorization.

> ²² Thus says the Lord God, "I will also take *a sprig* from the lofty top of the cedar and set *it* out; I will pluck from the topmost of its young twigs a tender one and I will plant *it* on a high and lofty mountain."
> ²³ "On the high mountain of Israel I will plant it, that it may bring forth boughs and bear fruit and become a stately cedar. And birds of every kind will nest under it; they will nest in the shade of its branches".
> ²⁴ "All the trees of the field will know that I am the Lord; I bring down the high tree, exalt the low tree, dry up the green tree and make the dry tree flourish."   Eze 17:22-24

- Note the italicized words that have been added. How does this stimulate your curiosity?
- What do you think are the key words in this passage?
- What is the impact of the imagery in these three verses?
- Do you see any symbolism? If so, what does it symbolize?

The cedars of Lebanon portray an image of being large and majestic. Note that the translators have added the word *sprig*. Without this additional word we have a more accurate translation. "God has taken from the lofty top of this majestic tree."

I suggest that the adjective describing the top of the tree is a key word. What is the "lofty top"? The verbal root for the Hebrew word that has been translated "lofty" is רוּם (*rum*), which means "high," or it can mean "exalted." Therefore, God seems to be selecting a small portion of the majestic tree, which is the new life at the top, and these few branches are exalted.

Listen again to Ezekiel 17:22 in its poetic rhythm. My translation follows.

> I will take from the exalted top of the cedar,
> And I will give [as an offering] from the tender head branches,
> And I will transplant it to a high and towering mountain.

The verb translated "I will give" simply means "to give." However, this verb is often used in connection with giving an offering to God. Therefore, this passage is conveying a subtle meaning about God's selection of exalted ones, and the purpose for that selection – a righteous offering to God.

If you read this verse aloud, you will hear the emotional rhythm, but also listen for the visual images. The topmost branches are new, light green, and tender. They are the new life. They are holy and worthy of sacrifice to God, and they are being transplanted from the mountains of Lebanon to Mount Zion in Jerusalem. As for symbolism, the towering cedar tree represents Israel,[11] but only the tender head branches are being selected and transplanted to Mount Zion.

There is another, equally important key word in our passage in Ezekiel. We have already identified my translation from the Hebrew as "exalted top of the cedar." Now consider the relationship between the three lines.

> I will take from the exalted top of the cedar,
> And I will give [as an offering] from the tender head branches,
> And I will transplant it to a high and towering mountain.

---

[11] Wood from the cedar tree was considered a holy and cleansing element (Lev 14:1-7, 48-57). The lofty cedar tree that grew in the mountains of Lebanon became the symbol for a righteous man (Lev 92:12). Zechariah 11:2 uses the cedar figuratively of fallen Israel.

We have three strong verbs – take, give, and transplant. I suggest that "exalted" in this passage refers to people, that is, some of God's people whom God has exalted. God is "taking" them [a form of selection], and "giving" them [as an offering because they are holy], and "planting" them on Mount Zion [where they will cultivate righteousness]. Why have I drawn this conclusion? In part because the Hebrew word for "head" in "tender head branches" is ראש (*rosh*), which is Hebrew for "head" that is a part of the body. In this context it literally means the head or top branches. However, *rosh* often refers to the heads of leaders of the clans and tribes of Israel. Thus, God is selecting these "heads" of the people. They are the exalted ones who are worthy to be selected as leaders.

Since the cedar tree represents Israel, God is making a selection from Israel in this passage in Ezekiel. However, given Matthew's use of this citation in the New Testament parable, I suggest that we can extend this concept to include a selection from all of God's people including Gentile believers in His son. One thing seems certain. Only the exalted ones at the top of the majestic tree are worthy in God's eyes. These are the ones who are apparently the leaders of God's people. I have concluded that they worthy to inherit the birthright, which is a special inheritance of leadership.[12] God will bring these exalted ones to Mount Zion at some time in the future where they will have a role to play in God's great plan of redemption.

Let us look now at the next verse, Ezekiel 17:23.

> On the high mountain of Israel I will plant it [the exalted top of the cedar tree], that it may bring forth boughs and bear fruit and become a stately cedar. And birds of every kind will nest under it; they will nest in the shade of its branches. Ez 17:23

---

[12] I have concluded, from my extensive work in Scripture, that God is selecting a remnant that will play a future role of leadership in defeating God's enemy. You can learn more about the remnant in my book on the parables where I cluster three parables together with one theme followed by a chapter on the remnant. I discuss fifteen parables, so there are five chapters on the remnant. Anne Kimball Davis, *Uncovering Mysteries in the Parables with Haggadic Midrash* (BibleInteract, 2013).

What to do with a Citation | 141

- In the first half of the verse, what seems to be the key word? Actually it is two words that convey one concept.
- Who bears fruit for God?
- Why are those who bear fruit for God exalted by Him?
- What is the relationship between the words "exalted" and "head" as they relate to the inheritance of the birthright?

Now it is time to turn back to the New Testament, but keep your finger in Ezekiel. Look again at the citation in the New Testament parable in Matthew that we have just seen in the second half of Ezekiel 17:23. In this comparison, you will note that the citation in the New Testament is not exactly the same as the verse it is citing. The ancient ear would have heard the difference, and in the intentional difference you will discover an exciting meaning.

THE BIRDS OF THE AIR come and NEST IN ITS BRANCHES. Mat 13:32

Birds of every kind will nest under it;
They will nest in the shade of its branches.
Ez 17:23b

I suggest that the ancient listener would have been startled because there is a striking difference between nesting *in* the branches, which I suggest represents the completion of God's work when His people will be at rest, and nesting *under* the shade of the branches. Nesting under the branches seems to represent loving protection.

- So consider now the question, "When do we need loving protection?"

We need it in our lives today. If we place ourselves in the loving protection of God, we have submitted in humble obedience to the Father through our faith in His son. If we are walking in the ways of the world, we have placed ourselves outside His loving protection unless, that is, we cry "help!" Then we must desire to repent (repent means "to change").

- Our next question must be, "Who do the birds represent?"

First consider the two physical objects. In Ezekiel we have already seen the topmost branches of the lofty cedar tree that God selected and exalted and transplanted to Mount Zion. Now we have birds that are nesting in the shade of the branches. I suggest that the exalted leaders are serving God by providing the protection of shade for God's people. The birds are God's people.

- Do you think the meaning of the parable in Matthew is related to "in the branches" or "under the shade of the branches," or could it be both? Explain your answer.
- Who do the branches represent? How do they provide shade and/or make a place for the birds?
- In Ezekiel 17:24, God has brought down the high tree ("high" represents pride) and has exalted the low tree ("low" represents humility). Who are the high and who are the low?

I suggest that nesting *in* the shade of its branches (Ezekiel) represents the end of God's work when all His children will be at rest in God's loving and comforting presence. The different words of the parable, nesting *under* the shade of the branches, would have startled the ancient listeners by the difference from what they had memorized in Ezekiel. Given the imagery of God selecting those who are worthy of leadership and transplanting them to Mount Zion, it seems that the branches, which provide shade, could signify the role of the remnant, those who serve God by leading His people. All the rest of God's people still belong to Him. However, they are not worthy to be exalted to the leadership role of the remnant, and are still in need of the protecting shade that God provides through His remnant.

Returning to the Parable of the Mustard Seed

It is time now to return to our parable in Matthew. Let me point out something else that is especially startling. The mustard plant in the parable is not a large and lofty tree like the cedar in Ezekiel. True, it has a small seed, but the plant is anything but lofty. The mustard plant is not a tree. It is a bushy and straggly plant that grows like a weed in Israel. You can find photos of it on the web if you choose.

What we seem to have, as we are learning about how to walk with God in His Kingdom, is that the Heavenly Father is making a selection of the tender tops (leaders of God's people) of the cedar tree (all of Israel extended by Matthew to all of His children) whom He is exalting. God's choice is not for the purpose of who will be saved and who will not be saved. Instead, He is selecting those who come to Him in humble obedience as they are being trained as leaders of God's people. They appear as a small, bushy, straggly plant to the world, but they are, in fact, humble and obedient before the power of God. They are towering and majestic trees in God's eyes.

Second Example of a Citation: All Israel will be Saved

We will now work through a second example of a citation. Paul cites Isaiah in Romans 11:26-27, and concludes from this citation that "All Israel will be saved" (Rom 11:26). Let us review what we must do when we see a citation in the New Testament.

- In the middle margin you will find what verse or verses Paul is citing. In this case, the middle margin leads us to Isaiah 59:20-21.
- Turn to Isaiah 59:20-21 and identify the context in which these two verses appear. The context will give us the probable memorized block that would have "flashed" in the minds of the ancient Israelites when they "heard" Paul's citation.
- Last, but certainly not least, compare what Paul has cited in Romans with the two verses in Isaiah. Are there any changes, additions, deletions, or anything startling that would have caught the attention of the ancient listener? If so, these will likely be clues to the deeper meaning that Paul is trying to convey.

We must remember that the Hebraic way of teaching and learning is very different from the Greek tradition that is prevalent in our western world today. So, here is a good place to "think

Hebrew, not Greek." You must resist elevating Paul as the authority by expecting him to tell you the correct interpretation. Instead, Paul is guiding you by giving you clues, so you will be able to discover the truth of God in His Word. This takes time and work, which is why only those with a heart to grow closer to God will probably uncover the mystery of this deeper meaning. I will now proceed in the Hebraic way of teaching by asking you questions.

- The cited verses are Isaiah 59:20-21, and the context seems to be Isaiah 59:15b-21. Therefore, carefully read this passage starting with "Now the Lord saw, and it was displeasing in His sight that there was no justice." What is the main idea of the context?
- Did you recognize the passage in Ephesians when you read Isaiah 59:17? The middle margin in Ezekiel will tell you where in Ephesians this echo occurs.
- In our passage in Ezekiel, God is prophesying something about the future. What is this prophecy?
- Who is the Redeemer who will come from Zion?
- To whom is the Redeemer coming? (Hint: see Ez 17:20).
- Carefully compare Isaiah 59:21 with Romans 11:27. What is startling? What has been added? What has been deleted?
- According to Paul in Romans 11:27, what part of the prophecy has been fulfilled? (Hint: Compare what Paul has added in his citation of Isaiah 59:21 with those to whom the Redeemer has come in Isaiah 59:20).
- By deleting the last part of Isaiah 59:21, Paul is apparently suggesting that this part of Ezekiel's prophecy has not yet been fulfilled. What, then, is still prophetic of something future for those of us today?
- Explain and describe how we only have the Spirit in part now.
- What will characterize the complete fulfillment of God's gift of the Spirit at some time in the future?

After you finish wrestling with these questions, you will be ready to return to ponder Paul's conclusion in Romans 11:26. "All Israel will be saved." From the context of this dramatic statement in Romans, you can see that this will happen sometime in the future "when the fullness of the Gentiles has come in." That in itself is puzzling, and I have never found a satisfying answer. However, there is a "mystery" that Paul *does* want you to uncover, and he has given you clues to be able to do that. By carefully answering the questions above you have started down the path of discovery. Paul is not going to give you a conclusive answer, nor am I. That is not the Hebraic way of teaching.

You might try to generate more of your own questions that will lead you deeper into this mystery. Try creating your own questions now before continuing to consider mine.

- What will be required for all Israel to be saved? (Hint: What did Paul add to his citation of Isaiah 59:22?)
- By deleting the last part of Isaiah 59:22, Paul was apparently explaining that this part of God's covenant was still future. Could this deletion also suggest *how* God will accomplish the salvation of all Israel? Explain your answer.

All Israel will be saved "after the fullness of the Gentiles has come in" (Rom 11:25). Does this necessarily mean before the Great Tribulation? Does it mean before the Millennial Kingdom? Does it mean during the Millennial Kingdom? Could it mean after the Millennial Kingdom? You must answer these questions with evidence from Scripture, not from your tradition or your gut feeling. If you do not have evidence from Scripture, you must reply, "I do not know." Perhaps this is a mystery you would like to uncover by using the ancient methods you have been learning in this course. [Hint: I suggest you will not uncover the answer all at once]. You will find that this adventure will be an unfolding process as you conduct your daily Bible study by using the ancient methods of uncovering deeper meaning.

Chapter Eleven
Connecting the Two Testaments

In my own work of searching the Scriptures I have concluded that the two testaments are not separate, nor is one merely the foundation for the other. Instead, both testaments are one unified message. We have already seen that the New Testament includes hundreds of citations and allusions to the Old Testament. Furthermore, New Testament authors frequently used language patterns characteristic of the Old Testament such as parallel lines, chiastic structure, and Hebraic idioms. Then there is the Hebraic way of teaching, which does not give answers but offers clues so a person can search to uncover a depth of meaning. Thus, the "Old" Testament is not merely a background and foundation for understanding and appreciating the "New" Testament. The New Testament is, in fact, a form of commentary on the Hebrew Scriptures. So, I suggest that the two testaments are intimately connected and cannot be separated.

We have already practiced this principle of connecting the two testaments when we worked on the Parable of the Mustard Seed that cited Ezekiel 17:23. Did you notice that we spent more time in Ezekiel than we did in Matthew? You have also seen an allusion to the Cain and Abel story when we were working on Paul's words, "no longer under law but under grace."

We will now continue to practice connecting the two testaments, this time by considering the language of judgment, which is prevalent in the Hebrew Scriptures. As a result, we tend to think of God as having condemned Israel through this language of judgment. There is almost none of this harsh language in the New Testament whose message appears to be one of God's love and grace. So, when we do encounter language of judgment in the New Testament we have trouble unraveling the meaning. In this session you will see that the language of judgment is a method of instruction that appears in both the Old and New Testaments (although more frequently in the Old). Furthermore, the message it conveys in both testaments is as relevant for us today as it was for the children of Israel before the coming of the Messiah and for those who first heard the gospel of Christ.

Introduction to the Language of Judgment

I will begin with some introductory comments. God's relationship with Israel is one of a Father (Dt 32:6), and Israel is His firstborn son (Ex 4:22). Thus, Scripture considers the people of Israel as children who belong to God. Nevertheless, some Christian interpretations suggest that only those children of Israel who believe in Yeshua, or who believed in the coming of God's promised Messiah, will be saved. After all, we hear Yeshua declare, "I am the way, and the truth, and the life; no one comes to the Father but through Me" (John 14:6). However, we must remember the Hebraic sense of time. Could it be that at some time in the future those with faith in Yeshua, both Jew and Gentile with past or future believing, will stand in righteousness before the Righteous God? I suggest that the theology that requires believing in Yeshua only in past or present time has contributed to the separation of the two testaments.

In the Hebraic sense of time, God created time so He *is* time and He exists in all aspects of time. His past promises are valid and become a reality when He first declares the promises, when the promises finally occur, and when we believe the promises today. Thus, "all Israel will be saved" is a prophetic promise, but Paul has brought it into our present experience as a certain reality. That is, according to the Hebraic sense of time the children of Israel belonged to God in the beginning. God gave them the Law to instruct them in righteousness so they could come into His presence, and they will come into God's presence in a righteous condition at some time in the future. But now, God has given to all mankind (both Jew and Gentile) His son. Therefore, not only do Jews belong to God as His firstborn son, but those Gentiles who believe in Yeshua also now belong to God. However, only those with faith in God's son (both Jew and Gentile) have the gift of the Holy Spirit to guide them in their walk of righteousness.

Paul appropriated this Hebraic sense of time when he cited creatively from Isaiah. First he added, "When I take away their sins," which is a future event. Yet, Paul has brought the future salvation of Israel into our consciousness as a present reality by declaring it as a certainty. "All Israel will be saved." Then, after Isaiah's words, "this is My covenant with them," Paul deleted the rest of the verse. Consider what Paul has deleted.

> "My Spirit which is upon you, and My words which I have put in your mouth, shall not depart from your mouth, nor from the mouth of your offspring, nor from the mouth of your offspring's offspring," says the Lord, "from now and forever."

By deleting these words Paul draws them to our attention. They speak of a future time when the Spirit of God will apparently have a role to play in God's promise, "all Israel will be saved."

I present this observation as a preface to our discussion about the language of judgment in the Hebrew Scriptures. The children of Israel knew they belonged to God, so their focus was on daily living. Thus, the language of judgment in the Hebrew Scriptures is a form of instruction directed toward God's people that encouraged them to walk in godly ways. This language has nothing to do with "being saved" or "not being saved." It is stern instruction for daily living, which helps God's children avoid the pain and suffering of the world caused by sin, and allows them to draw near to Him.

Compare this perspective about the children of Israel, who belong to God and need instruction in righteousness, with traditional Christian theology about salvation. Christianity focuses on "being saved." Thus, Christianity often leaves many questions unanswered. First, there are several interpretations about who will be saved and who will not be saved. The question of Israel's salvation is only one of these dilemmas. Another is whether believers in Christ must also make Yeshua Lord in their lives in order to be "saved." Then there is the predicament about defining belief in Christ. Are those who are bearing fruit for God the only ones who really believe?

Another troublesome problem in Christianity is the apparent difference between the God of the Old Testament and the God of the New Testament. In the Hebrew Scriptures God appears to be a God of wrath and judgment. The language sounds like God is condemning Israel so they no longer belong to Him. However, we will see that this is not language of condemnation but of loving instruction.

For believers in Christ, God is a God of love and grace. However, the New Testament God of love and the Old Testament

God of judgment are one and the same God. There is an interesting explanation. The children of Israel already knew they belonged to God because He declared He was their Father (Dt 32:6), and they were His firstborn son (Ex 4:22). Therefore, what they needed was instruction about walking in righteousness, which is why we have the language of wrath and judgment in the Hebrew Scriptures as a form of instruction for daily living. By contrast, Gentile believers in Christ hear God's language of love and grace because He has sent His son to make it possible for them to belong to Him. Furthermore, God has sent His gift of the Holy Spirit to both Jewish and Gentile believers in Christ so they can walk in His ways by their faith in His son. All of this exhibits God's grace and love.[13]

Working on the language of judgment will help you understand how the message in the Hebrew Scriptures about walking in righteousness, and the message in the New Testament about believing in Yeshua the Messiah, are actually one unified message, not two different covenants.

One God for Both Testaments

We will start with the understanding that God is not one to show partiality (Dt 10:17; Acts 10:34). He treats all His children the same, whether they are Jew or Gentile. Second, God instructs His children in numerous ways. He gave Israel the Law so the children of Israel would know *how* to walk in the ways of righteousness. He gave the Holy Spirit to believers in Christ so they *could* walk in the ways of righteousness with the help of the guiding Spirit. God also instructs His children through a process of "testing" (Ex 15:25; 16:24), which applies to both the children of Israel and to believers in Yeshua. God "tests" His children by allowing them to experience the consequences of their worldly actions (called

---

[13] We activate the gift of the Holy Spirit in us by walking in the same belief of God's son that first brought Gentiles into His family. As we continue to walk in that faith, we grow in the love of our Lord Yeshua who is guiding us into the presence of the Father.

"curses"). The purpose of testing is to encourage God's people to turn to Him, which leads to consequences (called "blessings").

I will now use the language of judgment in both the Old and the New Testaments to demonstrate that the two testaments are one unified message. Thus, messages in the Hebrew Scriptures are as relevant for believers in Christ as the New Testament gospel of Christ.

Characteristics of the Language of Judgment

There are two aspects of judgment. One is positive (rewards) and the other is negative (punishment). In daily living, both forms of judgment are for instruction. God uses the language of judgment to direct His people toward rewards, and one way of doing this is by threatening and inflicting punishment.

The biblical language of judgment (both positive and negative) is presented with extreme exaggeration and vivid imagery, which produces a sense of intense emotion and immediate urgency. Thus, the language of judgment is like an emotional carrot (the reward) and a stick (the punishment or correction). On one hand, God dangles the carrot and says, in essence, you will be with Me in peace and harmony and righteousness in a wonderful future kingdom. But beware of the stick! There will be consequences for your sinful actions.

We will now consider the language of judgment from the prophet Isaiah. Take time to answer the questions that follow.

> Sons I have reared and brought up,
> But they have revolted against Me.
> An ox knows its owner,
> And a donkey its master's manger,
> *But* Israel does not know,
> My people do not understand. Is 1:2-3

- Isaiah presents his message with the emotional rhythm of Hebrew poetry. Practice reading these verses aloud to capture this emotional rhythm.
- Which lines are in a parallel construction? What makes them parallel?

- Now carefully consider these parallel lines. What are the relationships between them?
- The language of prophecy uses vivid imagery. What is the imagery in this passage, and what message does it convey?
- The language of prophecy uses extreme exaggeration (a figure of speech called hyperbole). How is "revolting against God" extreme exaggeration?
- The last two lines are a summary conclusion that carries the message. What is the message?

I trust you have struggled with these questions yourself before considering my thoughts below.

The word "but" indicates a contrast, which shapes the message. Let me also share with you the way I viewed the parallel lines in this artistic structure.

> A. Sons I have reared and brought up,
> B. But they have revolted against Me.
> A. An ox knows its owner,
> A. And a donkey its master's manger,
> B. *But* Israel does not know,
> B. My people do not understand. Is 1:2-3

In the A lines, God is talking about the children He has raised. Did you recognize the metaphorical language that portrays two dumb animals, an ox and a donkey that exemplify the characteristics God is expecting of well-behaved children? He expects them to submit and obey. Now comes the "but" in the B lines. We turn from seeing God with His children to focusing solely on the disobedient children. Revolting against God in the first B line is followed by two parallel lines joined by Israel/My people and not know/not understand. Were you curious about the original Hebrew words translated "know" and "understand"? Could there be a slight difference in meaning? If so, what could that difference portray?

The message conveyed by Isaiah 1:2-3 is not restricted to Israel. The message applies as much to believers in Christ as it does to the children of Israel. When we do not know and when we do not understand, then we will sin. "Know" is ידי (*yada*), which implies knowing God's Word, and "understand" is בין (*bin*), which is to discern between good and evil. Therefore, without a strong knowledge of God's Word, and an ability to know the truth, we will be walking in the ways of the world and we will be revolting against God.

Isaiah continues.

> Alas, sinful nation,
> People weighed down with iniquity,
> Offspring of evildoers,
> Sons who act corruptly!
>
> They have abandoned the Lord,
> They have despised the Holy One of Israel,
> They have turned away from Him. Is 1:4

The extreme exaggeration is caused by repetition. I have a sense of being struck with a hammer. God is making certain His message hits home. The purpose of this intense language is to make us face our sinful nature and our ungodly actions. None of us are without sin. The language is stern, but the purpose is to encourage repentance. God wants His children to be one with Him, which they can only do when they are righteous, that is, without sin.

However, God does not leave us with this intense language of judgment, but turns to gentle, loving instruction.

> Wash yourselves.
> Make yourselves clean.
> Remove the evil of your deeds from My sight.
> Cease to do evil.
>
> Learn to do good.
> Seek justice.
> Reprove the ruthless.
> Defend the orphan.
> Plead for the widow. Is 1:16-17

- Read these verses aloud to capture the emotional rhythm.

154 | Recovering Ancient Methods of Bible Study

- Construct these verses in parallel lines using indents to display the artistic form and the relationships between the parallel lines.

- Now carefully consider the parallel lines. What is the artistic relationship between them?
- What message does each parallel construction convey?
- Describe the vivid imagery in this passage. What message does this imagery convey?
- What is the symbolism of washing, and what message does this symbol convey?
- What is the overall message of Isaiah 1:16-17 that we can put into our lives today?

Language of Judgment in the New Testament

We will turn now to the New Testament, which we tend to think contains only language of love and mercy. However, the New Testament also employs words of wrath and judgment, which many have concluded are directed toward Jews, not toward Christians. Let me show you that this is incorrect.

Connecting the Two Testaments | 155

We will consider a passage in the gospel of Matthew.

> Whoever causes one of these little ones who believe in Me to stumble, it would be better for him to have a heavy millstone hung around his neck, and to be drowned in the depth of the sea.
>
> Mat 18:6

Before we begin, note the setting in which Yeshua was speaking this extreme language. He was talking to his disciples (Mat 18:1)! At the time of Yeshua there were more disciples than just the inner circle of twelve (Acts 6:7). Furthermore, there are disciples among us today, disciples of their Master Yeshua. In fact, you are a disciple if you have made Yeshua Lord in your life, and you are committed to obey and serve him. Therefore, this strong language of judgment is directed toward all disciples of Yeshua, both in past times and also today. So, consider the following questions carefully.

- In the context of this verse (Mat 18:6), what have the disciples done to cause such a severe punishment?
- This passage is using extreme exaggeration to make a point. Imagine and describe death by suffocation caused by drowning.
- The purpose of the language is instruction in righteousness. How does this verse instruct the disciples in righteousness?

In the context of this account, the disciples of Yeshua were demanding to know, "who then is greatest in the kingdom of heaven?" (Mat 18:1). This grievous example of pride called for a stern reprimand. Yeshua then converts a strong rebuke into loving instruction. He called a child and set the child before his disciples. "Become like children," he admonished, but then he continues with the threat of a startling and horrifying punishment.

You will remember that extreme exaggeration is a figure of speech called hyperbole. So, you must not read the passage literally. That is, God causes no one to drown by suffocation, nor will this extreme situation ever be inflicted by God as a punishment. Instead, the harsh and graphic language conveys a message. Disciples must be very careful as they carry out the work of the

Lord. They must expel all pride from their thoughts and actions and teach humility by living a humble life. Humility never desires power or prestige or material possessions, so the disciple can identify completely with those in need.

The passage in Matthew then continues.

> If your eye causes you to stumble, pluck it out and throw it from you. It is better for you to enter life with one eye, than to have two eyes and be cast into the fiery hell.   Mat 18:9

Before posing questions for you to consider, let me explain "the fiery hell." The original Greek phrase means literally "the fire of Gehenna," which refers to the Hinnom Valley just south of Jerusalem where the garbage was brought to be burned. This is vivid imagery that essentially says, "Your actions are like stinking garbage and those actions need to be destroyed." It is another form of extreme exaggeration.

Now it is time for you to answer the following questions.

- This passage is using extreme exaggeration to make a point. Can you imagine having your behavior compared to burning garbage? What is there in your life that "stinks like garbage" and needs to be "thrown in the dump"?
- The purpose of the language is instruction in righteousness. How does the passage instruct the disciples to walk in righteousness?
- What does it mean to be righteous?

I have given you this example of the strong and seemingly condemning language of judgment in the New Testament to demonstrate the connection of the two testaments. We tend to identify this kind of harsh language exclusively with the Hebrew Scriptures, and think that God is treating Israel differently than He is treating believers in His son Yeshua. Not so. "God is not one to show partiality," but treats all His children alike (Dt 10:17; cf. Rom 2:11; Gal 2:6; Eph 6:9).

Connecting the Two Testaments

To fully appreciate the New Testament, you must have a solid foundation in the Hebrew Scriptures. The Torah is the central core of the Hebrew Scriptures, and I recommend that you become steeped first in the narrative portions of the Torah that you will find in Genesis, Exodus and Deuteronomy (Leviticus and Numbers are more legal in their approach and should be saved for more advanced work). Then you will be ready for the Prophets and the Writings.

However, do not overlook or skim over the New Testament. Even if you have studied the New Testament for years, you are now able to penetrate a greater depth of new and exciting meaning. Because of the Hebraic nature of the New Testament, you will be returning to the Hebrew Scriptures often.

Be prepared to conduct frequent word studies using the online interlinear Bible provided by biblehub.com. I guarantee that your life will change as you continue to conduct these word studies. You will draw closer to God through a growing understanding of the depth of His Word.

As only one example of uncovering this depth, consider Paul's words in his letter to the Galatians. The Law was "ordained through angels by the agency of a mediator, until the seed should come to whom the promises had been made" (Gal 3:19). Unfortunately interpretations have been made and theologies created without an adequate understanding of the relationship of these words to the Hebrew Scriptures. Consider the following questions below, and do your best to uncover the answers before considering my thoughts.

- How were angels involved when God gave the Law to the children of Israel at Mount Sinai?
- How was Moses a mediator, and why did Paul mention this role of a mediator?
- What is the promise, and where is this promise found in the Hebrew Scriptures?
- The Messiah is the "seed". How does Paul play artistically with the Hebrew word זרע (zera) in Galatians 3:16? (Hint:

zera, like the English word "sheep," uses a singular form to designate plural seed or descendants).

How many of these questions were you able to answer? How would you go about discovering the answers? If you wanted a deeper understanding, where would you begin? The purpose of recovering ancient methods is to give you the skills and the confidence to find your own answers to provocative questions rather than relying on interpretation offered by others.

We will now work together to unravel Paul's words in Galatians 3:16. We will start with angels, who were apparently messengers for God at Mount Sinai. There is no specific verse that gives us this information, but we can gather material that will help us. We will do this by letting Scripture interpret itself.

By using a concordance to see where "angels" appear in Scripture, you will discover that the presence of angels at Mount Sinai seems to have been a common understanding at the time of Yeshua. Consider the following:

- Stephen's words in Acts 7:53.
- The importance of God's Word in Hebrews 2:1-3.
- We also see that God communicated to John through an angel in Revelation 22:8.

> [8] I, John, am the one who heard and saw these things. And when I heard and saw, I fell down to worship at the feet of the angel who showed me these things.
> [9] But he said to me, "Do not do that. I am a fellow servant of yours and of your brethren the prophets and of those who heed the words of this book. Worship God."   Rev 22:8-9

You should not find the presence of messenger angels at Mount Sinai particularly surprising. We will never know for certain, but it is possible that the angel who spoke to Moses at the burning bush may have led the Jewish sages to conclude that angels would also have been present as messengers for God at Mount Sinai. So, we hear Paul declare, "The law was ordained through angels," which refers to a verse in Exodus.

> The angel of the Lord appeared to him [Moses] in a blazing fire from the midst of a bush; and he looked, and behold, the bush was burning with fire, yet the bush was not consumed. Ex 3:2

We turn now to Moses as mediator. Paul's point is that Jesus the Messiah needed no mediator. When Yeshua speaks, it is as though God is speaking. As for Moses, "A mediator is not for one," declares Paul, because God was speaking through an angel to Moses. So, there were two required to transmit information through Moses, God and an angel as Paul explains. "A mediator is not for one; whereas God is one." So, we see Yeshua who required no mediator. God spoke directly to His son, so the words from the Messiah carry greater power than the Law given to Moses through mediator angels.

What about "the promise"? Carefully read the passage that precedes our verse, which is Galatians 3:15-18.

- How is the promise related to a covenant?
- With which person did God make a covenant?
- The covenant extended to what other group of people? [Hint: See Galatians 3:6-9.]

You will find the original promise of inheritance in Genesis 17:1-5. The "multitude of nations," according to Paul, are the Gentiles (nations), who have been added to God's covenant by their faith in Christ.

Now we can turn to the promises that were spoken to "Abraham and his seed [descendants]." Paul is "playing artistically" with the Hebrew word זרע (*zera*), which takes only a singular form in Hebrew but conveys a plural meaning, which is similar to our English word "sheep." There can be one sheep or many sheep.

We started our search in the New Testament to understand Paul's words about angels. We asked the question, "How were angels involved when God gave the Law to Israel at Mount Sinai?" As we searched the Hebrew Scriptures to uncover the depth of what Paul is telling us, we discovered that Moses required the intermediary of an angel whereas Yeshua's words come directly from God. Because Yeshua, the son to whom God speaks directly, has greater authority than Moses, the servant who requires mediator angels, God's promise to Abraham could be fulfilled through His son. God has blessed the nations (Gentiles) by bringing them into a covenant relationship with Him through their faith in His son.

Conclusion

We have seen the connection of the two testaments in numerous ways. Citations in the New Testament lead us to the Hebrew Scriptures before we can return to the New Testament verse. Furthermore, the language of judgment may be prevalent in the Hebrew Scripture but it also appears in the New Testament. In both cases, God is using stern language to encourage repentance and a return to Him. Finally, we have seen a reference to "angels" that required our knowledge of the Hebrew Scriptures. This study has suggested through the Hebraic sense of time that God's children include the people of Israel and also Gentile believers in Christ. The Old Testament is not merely an historical and prophetic foundation to help us appreciate the gospel of Christ. Instead, the two testaments are intimately connected as one unified message.

Chapter Twelve
Stewards of the Mysteries of God

You have been learning to penetrate the depth of Scripture as people at the time of Yeshua would have searched the Scriptures to uncover its mysteries, to grow closer to God, and to answer difficult questions. They perceived the Holy Writings as communication from a loving God, and they turned to these writings to shape and regulate their daily lives.

If you have come this far in *Recovering Ancient Methods of Bible Study*, you have a deep desire to grow closer to God through the knowledge of His Word. In fact, you are a disciple of your Lord Yeshua. With what you have learned, together with the guiding work of the Holy Spirit, you will now be able to uncover mysteries in Scripture.

Paul's Words of Advice and Caution

As you penetrate an increasing depth of understanding, you will be taking on greater and greater responsibilities. God does not open hearts of understanding for no reason at all. As a worker for your Lord Yeshua, you will be serving God's people in a specific way that is calling you.

We will turn now to Paul, who offers poignant words regarding your participation in God's great plan to redeem His people and to bring them into His loving presence. Listen carefully to what Paul has to say.

> Let no one boast in men.... You belong to Christ, and Christ belongs to God. Let a man regard us in this manner, as servants of Christ and stewards of the mysteries of God.   1 Co 3:21, 23; 4:1

I suggest that you first consider and take to heart the striking repetition "Christ."

- You belong to Christ
- Christ belongs to God
- You are servants of Christ

Do you see the progression in these three statements? First you must belong to Christ by your faith in God's son. Then you grow in a relationship with Yeshua, who is leading you to the Father because "Christ belongs to God." Finally, you are ready to make Yeshua lord in your life so you can become a servant who is participating in the work of God.

Servants of Christ

There are three key words I would like you to consider – servants, stewards, mysteries. We will start with the role of a servant, who is dedicated to serve the Lord Jesus Christ.

Paul gives these words of advice. If God is going to reveal mysteries to you, then "let a man regard you as a servant of Christ." So, take time now to carefully consider the following verses that contain the word "servant." You should read each verse in its context in the Hebrew Scriptures, that is, within the surrounding verses that convey a full meaning of the word "servant."

- For each passage below, carefully consider what it means to be a servant of God. Then ask, "What is the relationship that God has with His servants?"

Genesis 18:3, 5	
Genesis 26:24	
Genesis 32:10	
Genesis 50:17, 18	

- Why do you think Scripture calls Moses a servant of God? Respond to this question in four steps.
    - (a) First, answer the question from your own perspective and understanding. (Don't skip this step; it is an important one).
    - (b) Second, read Numbers 12:7 in its context.
    - (c) Third, consider and compare your original answer from your tradition in (a) with what you have discovered in Numbers 12:7 (b).
    - (d) Finally, after completing your comparison, how might you change your original answer in (a)?
- The Exodus account offers a stark contrast between bondage to the ways of Satan and the world (represented by Pharaoh and Egypt) and humble service to God. Read the following verses in their context. Then describe the contrast between the two types of servitude, one to the world and the other to God.

Exodus 13:3, 14	
Exodus 14:12	
Exodus 16:3	
Exodus 17:3	
Exodus 20:2	

If you are going to pursue a study of Scripture to uncover its mysteries, you must be prepared to be a servant of God, and to understand from Scripture what this requires.

Stewards of the Mysteries

The Greek word that has been translated "steward" evokes a powerful word picture. The word is οἰκονόμος (*oikonomos*), which is the manager of a household, a very important position in ancient times that was normally held by the most faithful and trustworthy servant. Keep in mind that "servant" in the ancient world did not necessarily mean a slave. A servant was simply one who submitted to the authority of another. Paul urges you to become a faithful and trusty servant who will serve as a steward of God's household. How you carry out this responsibility will be a matter between you and your Lord.

Paul becomes our mighty mentor as we learn how to become stewards of God's people, and he shares with us his role as a steward. "I was made a minister [servant] according to the stewardship from God bestowed on me for your benefit, so that I might fully carry out the *preaching of the* word of God" (Col 1:25). Thus, one must be a servant first to become a steward of God's household. Paul then explains that his role as a steward was for the benefit of God's people.

As Paul continues in this passage, he offers us further understanding about his "*preaching of* the Word of God." This is the work he is doing as a steward. Note that *preaching of* has been added by the editors, so the focus is on the Word of God and the depth of meaning that Paul has uncovered and is teaching to God's people. Listen again to these words in Colossians.

> [25] ...the word of God,
> [26] *that is*, the mystery which has been hidden from the *past* ages and generations, but has now been manifested to His saints,
> [27] to whom God willed to make known what is the riches of the glory of this mystery among the Gentiles, which is Christ in you, the hope of glory.
> Col 1:25-27

Paul is sharing with God's people a mystery that he has discovered from the depth of Scripture that God has made known to him. This is not the only mystery. As you study the New Testament, you will find references to other mysteries that have been uncovered and proclaimed as well. Nevertheless, Paul's mystery, which is "Christ in you," is a powerful understanding that could easily become an entire study in its own right. We will not take time to do that study. I simply want you to understand that those who are serving under the lordship of Yeshua, and are becoming stewards of God's people, will be uncovering mysteries that God expects them to share.

You are learning how to uncover these mysteries. You will remember that people of ancient Israel believed that God was the author of His Word, and that He had offered not only a plain and simple message but also a deeper meaning they called "mysteries." Listen again to Paul talking about these mysteries.

> We speak God's wisdom in a mystery, the hidden *wisdom* which God predestined before the ages to our glory. 1 Co 2:7

By "we" Paul means those who have become his disciples, and there are mysteries that have been hidden in the depth of God's Word. God has determined when these mysteries will be disclosed, so Paul can express them as predestined. That is, in the Hebraic sense of time the mysteries have existed from the beginning, but now God is calling you to uncover these mysteries.

"To You it has been Granted to Know the Mysteries"

Let us turn now to the Parable of the Sower and the Seed where Yeshua talks to his disciples about these mysteries. You may have encountered this discussion of the parable in my book, *Uncovering Mysteries of the Kingdom: Viewing the Parables as Haggadic Midrash*. Nevertheless, I would like to include similar information here because it summarizes the work we have been doing on recovering ancient methods of Bible study.

We learn that "Yeshua was sitting by the sea, and great multitudes gathered to him." He told them the Parable of the Sower and the Seed (Matthew 13:1-9). When Yeshua had finished speaking to the multitudes, the disciples came to him and asked, "Why do you speak to them in parables?" Yeshua answered with these words. "To you [disciples] it has been granted to know the mysteries of the kingdom of heaven, but to them [the multitudes] it has not been granted" (Mat 13:11).

We will begin by listening to the parable as the multitudes would have heard it.

- Carefully read Matthew 13:1-9.
- Listen for repetition. How does the repetition prompt you to ask questions?

When we "listen" to the parable as the multitudes would have heard it, the first thing we notice is repetition. "The sower went out to sow; and as he sowed..." Certainly this gives us a rhythm that is characteristic of the biblical language, but the ancient ear would also have heard the repetition. So, we ask, "Is this repetition of sowing a clue? If so, could it be alluding to a concept of sowing in the Hebrew Scriptures?" After all, we are trying to "hear" the ancient text the way the people of the first century would have heard it.

There is another repetition that is even more provocative because the conclusion of the parable repeats, "Others fell on the good soil, and yielded a crop, some a hundredfold, some sixty, and some thirty. He who has ears, let him hear" (Mat 13:8-9; repeated in Mat 13:23). Let us begin with the repetition of sowing.

The three-letter root for sowing in Hebrew is זרע (*zarah*) from which various related words can be constructed including a verb (to sow) and a noun (what is sown, which is seed). The noun appears often in the biblical text and is used to convey "offspring" or "descendants". For example, God told Abraham, "All the land that you see I will give to you and your offspring [seed] forever" (Gen 13:15). "Seed" or "offspring" is the noun form of זרע, to sow seed.

The first time זרע is used in its verbal construct is in Genesis 26:12. "Now Isaac sowed in that land and reaped in the same year a hundredfold. And the Lord blessed him." Stop! Do you hear something in Genesis 26:12 that the Parable of the Sower is echoing? If not, return to the parable in Matthew and "listen."

As you continue considering the parable in Matthew 13:1-9 you will see five methods of sowing seed. Before continuing, consider the first four categories that represent four groups of people.

- Seeds fell beside the road, and the birds came and ate them up.
- Seeds fell upon the rocky places, where they did not have much soil; and immediately they sprang up, because they had no depth of soil.
- When the sun had risen, they were scorched; and because they had no root, they withered away.
- Others fell among the thorns, and the thorns came up and choked them out.

All four methods of sowing seed failed to yield a crop. However, the fifth method sowed on good soil, and the result was seed that grew to be harvested. Metaphorically speaking, this seed is bearing fruit for God. However, the yield on the good soil is not uniform. Listen to the three categories of yield on the good soil.

- Some yielded a crop that was a hundredfold.
- Some yielded a crop that was sixty.
- Some yielded a crop that was thirty.

As you continue to listen to the parable, you will hear this last method of sowing repeated. Those whose seed fell on good soil "yielded a crop, some a hundredfold, some sixty, and some thirty. He who has ears, let him hear" (Mat 13:8-9; repeated in Mat 13:23). This repetition is the clue that will lead us to the Hebrew Scriptures.

A Crop that Yielded a Hundredfold

We turn now to the repetition, "Some yielded a crop that was a hundredfold." By using a concordance you will learn that in Genesis 26:12 Isaac sowed and reaped a hundredfold.

I encourage you to work on this passage in Genesis first before considering my thoughts. You should begin by reading

Genesis 26:12 in its context, which I suggest is Genesis 26:1-17. You should stop now and follow this principle of reading Genesis 26:12 in its context before continuing. Then ponder the following questions.

- What verses comprise the context of Genesis 26:12?
- Why did Isaac go to Gerar, to Abimelech king of the Philistines? How does this action by Isaac form a contrast to the abundance of his later reaping a hundredfold? Why is this contrast important to the inner sense of the story in Genesis?
- As you read through this account, what did Isaac do? That is, what were his actions that led to God's blessing him?
- What is the symbolism of three words that relate agricultural activities to godly ways of living - seed, sowing, reaping?
- Why did Isaac tell Abimelech that Rebekah was his sister? What are several possible scenarios of what *might* have happened as a result of this seemingly deceitful act? What *actually* happened? How do you explain the outcome?
- Why did God bless Isaac with such an extraordinary abundance of crops?
- "A hundredfold" is likely an exaggeration for the purpose of emphasis, which is a linguistic device called hyperbole. What is hyperbole, and how is it functioning in this verse?

Because of a famine in the land of Canaan, Isaac moved his flocks and possessions to Gerar, the area around Beersheba. To prevent Abimelech, the king of Gerar, from killing Isaac so he could take his beautiful wife Rebekah, Isaac declared that Rebekah was his sister. When Abimelech finally discovered that Rebekah was Isaac's wife, he demanded an explanation from Isaac who replied, "lest I die on account of her." What follows is significant.

> [11] So Abimelech charged all the people, saying, "He who touches this man or his wife shall surely be put to death."
> [12] Now Isaac sowed in that land and reaped in the same year a hundredfold. And the Lord blessed him,
> [13] and the man became rich, and continued to grow richer until he became very wealthy.
>
> Gen 26:11-13

I suggest that Isaac feared for his life, so God responded by allowing Isaac to live instead of facing death at the hand of Abimilech. This act by God represents the gift of life that God gives to all His children. Then God blessed Isaac again by bestowing abundance in his daily life with sowing and reaping. As we reflect on Isaac's yield of a hundred fold, we realize that God gives these same two things to all His children – the promise of eternal life with Him, and abundance in our daily lives *if* we submit and obey.

However, the most important concept I see in this passage is that Isaac responded to a famine, which represents the trials and tribulations of the world. God only blesses us in our daily lives when we respond to inevitable trials and tribulations in godly ways. Isaac was humble and obedient in his life with God, who blessed him with abundance.

- How does this account of Isaac in Gerar help you understand how to live as disciples of Yeshua?
- What will be at least one of your rewards (other than eternal life with God)?

In the parable, those who sowed on good soil yielded a crop that was a hundredfold. This startling connection to Isaac in the Hebrew Scriptures is followed by Yeshua announcing, "He who has ears, let him hear," which is going to become significant in our understanding of the parable because, before Yeshua delivered the "explanation" to his disciples, he cited a passage from Isaiah about "deaf ears" and "failing to hear." Yeshua *wants* his disciples (and we are disciples if we have a heart to hear) to go deeper than the understanding of the multitudes. Are you going to be part of the crowd, or are you going to penetrate the depth of what Yeshua is trying to tell you?

Continuing to Search the Hebrew Scriptures

We have seen the connection of reaping a hundredfold in Genesis 26:12 where Isaac sowed an abundance described as a hundredfold. The parable in Matthew continues. Those whose seed fell on good soil "yielded a crop, some a hundredfold, some sixty, and some thirty" (Mat 13:8). So we ask, "Could there be a connection to the Hebrew Scriptures for sixty and thirty as well?" Before returning to the Hebrew Scriptures, consider the following.

- Do you think that yielding a crop that is sixty and thirty-fold will appear somewhere in the Hebrew Scriptures?
- If so, where are you likely to find it?
- How will you look for these words in the Hebrew Scriptures?

A concordance will tell you where the numbers sixty and thirty appear in Scripture. I suggest you do your own work first before reading what I have discovered. You will need to scan through the various verses in a concordance that list where the Hebrew words sixty and thirty appear. Then select the two verses with ששים and שלשים that seem to relate to the story in the parable.

We turn now to the number sixty. As I searched in a concordance I followed the principle that would have been characteristic of first century thinking, that all major concepts in the Hebrew Scriptures will likely appear first in the Torah. The number sixty appears in only four passages in the Torah: Genesis 25:26; Leviticus 27:3, 7; Numbers 7:88; Deuteronomy 3:4. I selected Genesis 25:26 as the most likely verse to which the parable is referring, which happens to be its first occurrence. There we learn that when Rebekah bore twin sons to Isaac (Esau and Jacob), "Isaac was sixty years old when she gave birth to them." Scripture does not identify the age of a person unless there is some significance. Furthermore, numbers in Scripture have symbolic meaning.

If you refer to the classic work for explaining the symbolism of numbers, which is *Number in Scripture* by E. W. Bullinger, you will discover that the number sixty is six multiplied ten times for emphasis, so six is the number we need to scrutinize.

Bullinger explains that the number six is generally related to the world. However, he also points out something I think is relevant to our parable. Explains Bullinger, "*Man* was created on the *sixth* day... Moreover, *six* days were appointed to him for his labour; while *one* day is associated in sovereignty with the Lord God, as His rest. *Six*, therefore, is the number of *labour* also, of man's labour as apart and distinct from God's rest [italics are Bullinger's]." Thus, a follower of the Lord Yeshua is called to be a servant to work for the Master. This labor is the work of service, which is an important requirement for disciples. The parable is continuing to instruct us how to serve as disciples of the Lord Yeshua. Committed followers of Yeshua are expected to work for him; he is their Lord. I suggest that this concept of working for God is the significance of bearing sixtyfold in the parable.

We turn now to the number thirty. I believe the verse with the strongest evidence for a connection to our parable is Genesis 41:46. "Joseph was thirty years old when he entered the service of Pharaoh, king of Egypt." The key concept continues to be serving the Lord, which is not surprising since Yeshua was talking to his disciples.

We know that a disciple serves his master, so who was Joseph serving? Our answer lies in the symbolism of Joseph as a "type" of Christ, and Pharaoh as the authority over Joseph. The Pharaoh represents God the Father. So Joseph, who is a type of Christ, serves the Pharaoh, who symbolizes God the Father. Yet, there is more. Joseph so excelled in humble obedience that God declared him worthy to claim the inheritance of the birthright that bestows a leadership role (1 Chron 5:1-2).

This powerful imagery extends beyond Joseph to disciples who serve their Lord and Master, Yeshua the Messiah, who then leads them to the higher authority of God the Father. So, this verse about Joseph seems to be the echo for our parable. Joseph was thirty years old when he entered the service of the Pharaoh, which was considered the age of maturity in the ancient world. We can also enter the service of our master when (and if) we reach spiritual maturity.

So, our parable concludes that those whose seed falls on good soil "yield a crop, some a hundredfold, some sixty, and some thirty." A hundredfold is the crop we bear for God despite the times of famine and hardship that all of us must experience. Sixty is the crop that produces new life, which is the new creation that we become when we walk in righteousness. Thirty is the final step and ultimate goal. God selects those He considers worthy to lead His people both now and sometime in the future when they will claim the special inheritance known as the birthright. Yeshua is encouraging his disciples to be dedicated followers who labor in the service of their Master in order to bear fruit for God.

Disciples of the Lord Yeshua

Following the parable in Matthew 13:1-9, we see two distinct sections. First is the citation from Isaiah 6:9-10 with accompanying commentary (Mat 13:10-17). We remember that we must compare the citation in the New Testament with what it cites in the Hebrew Scriptures. If there seems to be a significant difference, it may be for the purpose of conveying a deeper meaning.

> MATTHEW: [15] YOU WILL KEEP ON HEARING, BUT WILL NOT UNDERSTAND; YOU WILL KEEP ON SEEING, BUT WILL NOT PERCEIVE.
> [16] FOR THE HEART OF THIS PEOPLE HAS BECOME DULL, WITH THEIR EARS THEY SCARCELY HEAR, AND THEY HAVE CLOSED THEIR EYES, OTHERWISE THEY WOULD SEE WITH THEIR EYES AND HEAR WITH THEIR EARS; AND UNDERSTAND WITH THEIR HEART. Mat 13:15-16

> ISAIAH: [9] Go, and tell this people: 'Keep on listening, but do not perceive; Keep on looking, but do not understand.'
> [10] Render the hearts of this people insensitive, their ears dull, and their eyes dim. Otherwise they might see with their eyes, hear with their ears, understand

> with their hearts, and return and be healed."
> Is 6:9-10

I see no significant difference between the citation spoken by Yeshua when compared to the passage in Isaiah. If this is so, then the purpose of the citation is a "prooftext." That is, something prophesied in the Hebrew Scriptures was taking place in the time of Yeshua. In this case, many of God's people were unable to know the mysteries of the kingdom of heaven because they were not committed followers of the Master. Nevertheless, there were some who were obedient in the same way that Isaac was obedient. They were working for God as the number sixty represents. They were serving in the service of God as Joseph was serving his master the Pharaoh. These are the disciples.

God wants these disciples to uncover the mysteries of the kingdom of God, so Yeshua concludes the citation of Isaiah with these encouraging words.

> Blessed are your eyes because they see; and your ears because they hear. For truly I say to you that many prophets and righteous men desired to see what you see, and did not see *it;* and to hear what you hear, and did not hear *it.*" Mat 13:16

What were the disciples seeing and hearing? They were seeing and hearing the mysteries of the kingdom of heaven. What can you see and hear if you are a disciple or follower of your Lord? Yeshua delivered every parable in such a way that the multitudes would hear a simple story. However, the disciples can work to follow the clues that will lead them to uncover the deeper meaning.

There is a final distinct section that follows the citation from Isaiah, which appears in Matthew 13:18-23. The title for this section in the New American Standard Bible declares, "The Sower Explained." However, the deeper meaning of the parable goes far beyond what we read in Matthew 13:18-23. The enticing clue to the deeper meaning is the repetition of the powerful words about yielding a hundredfold, sixty and thirty in the concluding verse Matthew 13:23. "The one whose seed was sown on the good soil, this is the man who hears the word and understands it; who indeed bears fruit, and brings forth, some a hundredfold, some sixty, and some thirty" (Mat 13:23). If you compare Matthew 13:23 with what it repeats from Matthew 13:8-9, you will see that something has been added. The ancient ear would have heard this expansion.

- Compare Matthew 13:8-9 and 13:23. What has been added?
- What is the difference between "hearing" the Word of God and hearing it with your heart?
- What are the requirements for you to "understand" the Word of God?
- What is the relationship between hearing and understanding?
- Are you hearing the Word of God and understanding, or are you simply hearing?

We must not forget the first four groups whose seed failed to bear fruit. These are the multitudes who hear but do not understand, and see but do not perceive. These people came to hear Yeshua teach, but they were not disciples. They were not obeying God and laboring in His service. Therefore, they were not bearing fruit for God. They were not capable of comprehending the mysteries of the kingdom of heaven. Disciples, on the other hand, have hearts that truly desire to grow close to God, and they are eager to do the work that the clues are stimulating.

Conclusion

As you continue to search the Scriptures using these ancient methods, your knowledge and understanding of Scripture will grow at an amazing rate. Far more important, this knowledge will lead you to God, and to an understanding of what He is doing and the role He is asking you to play.

Your life will grow in abundance. We learn this from the words of Yeshua who explained, "Whoever has, to him *more* shall be given" (Mat 13:12). You must take the responsibility of your knowledge and understanding wisely. You must use it to serve your Lord Yeshua as a faithful servant. If you do not, then remember the words that Yeshua directed to his disciples. "Whoever causes one of these little ones who believe in Me to stumble, it would be better for him to have a heavy millstone hung around his neck, and to be drowned in the depth of the sea (Mat 18:6)." These are not words of condemnation, but strict instruction. The instruction is delivered as hyperbole using the language of judgment and wrath.

The choice is yours. I trust you will choose a life of abundance as a servant of your Lord Yeshua and as a steward of the mysteries of God.

Epilogue
Further Study

The Hebraic way to study is in community, so dialogue and discussion become a major part of the learning process. Therefore, BibleInteract offers a program on "Recovering First Century Methods" with twelve DVD lectures by Dr. Anne Davis. Each lecture covers much of the material found in the chapters of this book, but there is also a workbook that accompanies the lectures. This workbook is designed for small group study, or for work with a study partner.

Each workbook chapter includes the following sections:
- Summary of the session
- Outline of the lecture (recommended for taking notes and organizing your thoughts)
- Words to be defined
- Questions for Comprehension
- Building Skills
- Questions for Discussion
- Digging Deeper
- Application Questions

An important part of each of the twelve workbook chapters is entitled "Building Skills." The program begins with basic proficiency, and then continues to build more complex and advanced skills that use ancient methods of searching the Scriptures.

Another essential element of the workbook includes less difficult and more difficult activities. The leader of the group should assess the level of the group's ability, and select those exercises that best fit the nature of the group.

Finally, the most important requirement for learning how to uncover the mysteries of Scripture, and to penetrate its depth of meaning, is to allocate frequent time for Bible study. You must do the work that is required. Start with your curiosity, and then use all the skills you have learned in this program. As you apply what you are learning, you will grow increasingly into a new creation. You will slowly change to become the "new man," and you will begin to walk as Jesus Christ walked. You will be doing the work of your Lord, and you will become a steward of God's household.

BibleInteract also offers continuing study of the Scriptures that employ the ancient methods of Bible study. These courses include such portions of the Bible as Genesis, Isaiah, Romans and Galatians, and come with DVD lectures and workbooks. The instructor explains how these ancient methods are being used, and shares thoughts and conclusions. However, the heart of the program continues to be group discussion and dialogue. You will be learning and practicing how to use ancient methods to uncover a depth of meaning.

For more information, visit the BibleInteract website – http://bibleinteract.com.

Printed in Great Britain
by Amazon